W0009287

Distributed in the United Kingdom by

Amountainbivvy Publishing

ISBN 9798448440533

This book is dedicated to my children Will and Annie.
May you find in life treasure that has real value.

Index

The mountains are listed in alphabetical order

Prologue
Lake District - September 2019

Once you have slept on a mountain you connect with it differently than if you have just climbed to the top. Nan knew this, Alfred almost did, he spent the nights but not the sleep and it was confirmed to me one day when fell running from Dubbs Road to Kirkstone Pass. This was back in September 2019 and running with Gambus it was a wet windy day with the sun breaking through on occasion. Gel sachets in pockets and watches synced we left Garburn Pass and climbed up Yoke, the view over to Troutbeck Tongue was obscured by clag. Nearing the top, a warm feeling of nostalgia came over me. 'I've bivvied there,' I excitedly pointed to him. It was the first words I'd managed in twenty minutes of puffing. 'Just there, between the summit crag and the wire fence'.

He looked at the spot. 'That bit with all the sheep poo?'

'Yes, the sheep always know the best spots for a sleep'. We carried on running, up and down over Ill Bell, up and down over Froswick, and then on Thornthwaite Crag the nostalgia feeling came over me again. 'I've bivvied there,' I told him a bit more tiredly this time, 'behind that wall sheltering from the wind'.

'Really?' was half an answer and half a statement that he wanted to get on with the running.

'Yes, one day when I was hiking a loop around Patterdale with Martin and we ....' I must have been boring him.

'I'll see you back at the van, I know the way,' and he was off leaving me to my memories.

Threshwaite Crag is a delightful climb and once he was out of sight I stopped and walked a bit, no longer feeling the pressure to keep up with him anymore. He would have to wait for me at the van as I had the keys. Descending from Stoney Covey Pike I got that nostalgia feeling for the third time. I recognised the spot I had camped on once in the snow. Not on the summit but just a small flat grass patch under a rocky crag. I knew then that there was definitely something special about Wild Camping on the mountain. You don't really know a mountain until you have slept on it, and once you have, you forever view it as a friend.

How to read this book

Cramming a year's worth of adventure and a lifetime's wisdom into one book is not easy, which is why I have split it into four books, one for each season. Now it's finished it's for you to decide how to read this book.

You can read from the first page to the last and feel like you are coming along on my journey, immersed in mountain scenery, enjoying, and battling the conditions in equal measure. Moving through the seasons and sleeping on the mountain tops.

Alternatively, as each page is one day on one mountain they can be read as a standalone short story. Designed not to be a detailed guide but to give you a feel of the mountain, pick out some of the highlights and give you an idea of what it is like to camp on. Flick through to find inspiration for your next adventure.

The final option is for those like me who enjoy randomness. You can put all 214 Wainwright Fell names into a bag, I recommend a yellow one and pick them out one mountain at a time. This way your experience of reading the book will be unique and show you a perspective that no one else has. Reading the book this way gives more variations than there are atoms in the Universe.

Whichever way you choose to read this book, do it slowly so you can savour the mountains.

Mountain Sleep Bagging

Origins

If a name is to be given to the activity I am engaged in, then Mountain Sleep Bagging seems to describe it well. The origins come from two quotes that inspired me and are worth repeating.

Nan Shepherd 'No one knows the mountain completely who has not slept on it. As one slips over into sleep, the mind grows limpid; the body melts; perception alone remains. Those moments of quiescent perceptiveness before sleep are among the most rewarding of the day. I am emptied of preoccupation, there is nothing between me and the earth and sky.'

Alfred Wainwright. 'One of the best ways to avoid other people is to spend the night there. Once you have spent the night on the mountain you are never again awed by it but view it with affection.'

I suppose you could say Nan and Alfred are the parents of Mountain Sleep Bagging and I am their firstborn offspring.

Rules

Now the activity has a name I suppose it also needs rules. There are only two rules I have used during my yearlong adventure 1) I must reach the top of the mountain. 2) I must sleep the night on the mountain. Reaching the top normally takes place before the sleeping but on the odd occasion, I reached the summit the following morning before going back down. This happened a couple of times on the Bob Graham Round five-night excursion. Sleeping on the mountain can be anywhere on the mountain. It's often confused with sleeping exclusively on the summit, but if you have gone to all the effort of climbing to the top why would you then go back down to sleep. Only in severe weather did I sleep lower down and then it still had to be acceptable with the Wild Camping guidelines. Sleeping on the shoreline next to Buttermere and claiming you have slept on High Stile won't cut the mustard. There is no prize for this activity, other than your own personal reward, so in the end, you are the judge of your achievements. It's only you and the mountain that know if you have that special connection.

Rewards

I think of Mountain Sleep Bagging as an expression of art, adventure art you could call it. The rewards come from the experience. I saw amazing sunrises, red translucent fireballs rising behind Blencathra in the morning revealing the earth as its true self. Stormy sunsets over Ennerdale where the sky turned metallic purple and orange and the light reflecting on the lake made it look like melted gold. There were times in raging snowstorms when apart from my red nose, white was all I could see and other days when the drops of rain hanging on the tent looked like crystals. There was so much beauty it had to be Art.

My Round

I chose to use the 214 Wainwrights for my Sleep Bagging Adventure in part because I had been inspired by the great fell running stories of the Lake District. I remember seeing Steve Birkinshaw race the clock down to set his record at Moot Hall. He became the first person to run around all the Wainwrights in under a week. The difference with my round though is it wasn't a race against time, it took 214 nights to sleep on all the Wainwrights, and for the next person to complete a round this way it will also take them 214 nights. The adventure was not about going faster or further than before. The adventure was the journey and there was no competition.

Tempted to try mountain sleep bagging?

Aristotle said 'The whole is greater than the sum of its parts' I don't know if he was a wild camper, but his phrase describes beautifully what mountain sleep bagging gives you that wild camping on its own doesn't. I can tell you this, but it is not until you go and try it for yourself that you will really understand.

Mountain Sleep Bagging Rounds Ideas (number of nights needed in brackets)

The National Three Peaks (3)
The Yorkshire Three Peaks (3)
The Scottish 4000s (9)
The Welsh 3000s (15)
The Wainwrongs (55)
The Ethels (95)
Pyrenean 3000s (126)
All the Welsh Mountains (189)
The Wainwrights (214)
The Munros (282)

Base Van Camp

Base Van Camp is my trusted companion on my adventure, and I have even come to think of it as having a voice of its own.

'Bivvybagging! I don't see what is so special about that. It's just spending the night outside in a waterproof bag like rubbish does. @amountainbivvy tells me that simplicity is the ultimate sophistication, and the simplest form of wild camping is bivvybagging. I tell him then; in that case, he also is ultimately sophisticated. Because he is definitely simple. I don't see what the attraction is of lying on the ground in a bag and sleeping. He loves the idea of persuading others to try sleeping in the open and dreams one day of being a world record holder for bivvybagging. He'll never get me to try it, that's for sure. Although there are others which I know he will be able to persuade.'

Bivvybagging

For those that don't know, a Bivvybag is a waterproof bag that goes over your sleeping bag and that is all there is to it. You don't need a tent and can fall asleep with stars for a blanket.

For those that do know, a Bivvybag can bring more happiness, reward, and satisfaction than any other type or style of bag in existence. Apart from of course, Yellow Bag.

Yellow Bag

I sit in the cupboard
It's dark
I only get let out once a day,
I have friends in here
The OS maps of the Lake District
Dobble
And a few books to read.
The Alchemist, about a shepherd finding treasure.
I know where the treasure is
It's on the mountain tops at night
He never takes me
I don't mind
I'm just a bag
In the dark
In a cupboard

Summer

'One night's exposure in the mountains is better than reading a cartload of books' John Muir

Base Van Camp: 'The mountains have been his medicine. He no longer feels depressed and is loving life in the mountains, living as a mountain hermit. "This is my happy place; this is where I belong" he says into the camera on the top of Grasmoor for a news piece on the BCC. It was one of his favourite camps and made for great TV. The sun rising in the morning was below the mountain and appeared as a red fireball, not the yellow circle you see in the midday. My view next to the boulder in Braithwaite wasn't quite as good, but still enjoyable. The trouble is, it is not real life, or at least not a life that can continue indefinitely. At some point, he is going to have to return to earn a living. In the beginning, getting to the starting line was his focus. He needed to escape real life, get some distance otherwise if his dreams of death bivouac had come true it would have been a sad ending. He was being tortured by the mundane. Now he is loving the camping and wants to make sure he can finish.

He attends an Independent Medical Examination over Zoom, I make a comfy seat for him in the back of the van. He explains the situation and the doctor understands. Returning to work now would likely cause a return to the negative feelings he was suffering from before the start of the adventure. He feels he needs the option of returning to work at some point, it's like a safety net, it's all he has done for 17 years. It's a case of Stockholm syndrome and he doesn't know what else he could do. He has always struggled with other people and has been happy in his own company. You are never alone with that many voices in your head. The doctor is happy for him to continue his camping but recommends he sees a psychiatrist to obtain a diagnosis for why he has outbursts of anger when around others.'

Grey Knotts - 697 metres
Western Fells – 1st June

The Adventure - Pixie

Grey Knotts from Honister Pass makes for the quickest walk to the summit. I'm on my own and it's a sad day, Pixie my dog, a Cavalier King Charles Spaniel had to be put to sleep. In times like this, an escape to the mountains helps put it all in perspective. She always loved the mountains. Some days she wouldn't walk fifty meters down the street but bring her to the mountains and she would happily walk ten miles. Cross Fell in the Pennines and Goat Fell on Arran were two of the biggest she had climbed. It would have been nice if she had accompanied me on one of my camps, but she had been too ill from the start. As the evening draws in the North Star is the first to appear in the still blue sky above Innominate Tarn. I say a prayer to whoever is listening, knowing that she will always be with me in my memory and heart. The orange horizon gradually fades into an inky blue and the tarn reflects the last of the light surrounded by dark mountains. I sit, doing nothing but watching the landscape feeling wild awake.

The Mountain Camp

Steep and of no particular interest is the path from the top of Honister pass. It's even more ugly when you turn around to look at the view and see the Quarry Road going to the top of Fleetwith Pike. Despite the steepness, it still manages to hold onto water which makes it also boggy. The advantage is a quick route to the top as I have saved myself 350 metres of climbing. A much nicer walk would have been from Seathwaite following Newhouse Gill, passing the old graphite mine and into Gillercomb Valley. The Plumbago mines, as they were called in previous centuries had many uses, from marking sheep, lining moulds for cannon balls, and making pencils. Keswick is world famous for its pencil museum. The route up the Eastern side brings out the best in Grey Knotts and there are many great rock and boulder climbs amongst the crags. On the summit, there is an ugly wire fence running through the middle of it and the cairn has barely ten stones in it. However, the best reason to visit and the highlight of this fell is when you pass over the top, reach the next set of crags, and look towards Haystacks. The view is amazing, sweeping from Great Gable all the way to Robinson in a magnificent panorama of the very biggest and best mountains. I pitch my tent on a fabulous rock alter with crags all around and watch the sun glow red as the day ends.

Shipman Knotts - 587 metres
Far Eastern Fells – 2nd June

The Adventure – True Summit

Last time I didn't get to the top. Three years later my mistake is to be rectified as I climb up from Sadgill, cross over the River Sprint on the pretty little pack horse bridge, and head through Sadgill wood. Following the unnamed pass between Longsleddale and Kentmere I turn off at the highest point and this time stick to the east to the side of the wall. There is no path, I'm going off track and it is making this fell a lot more enjoyable. The ground is uneven grass with hummocks and the drystone wall leads all the way to the summit and beyond. It's a warm day and time is on my side. At the summit, there is no stile across the wall in either direction for at least half a mile. The cairn on the western path isn't the true summit. This is on the eastern side of the wall where there is no path. This makes me question as to what counts as reaching the true summit? Is it if you stand on the highest point? Or just touch it? Is it if your head is higher than the highest point? Is it a five-metre area surrounding the mountain top? There is no definite right answer. On mountains like Helm Crag the highest point is a rock climb and Wainwright didn't even bag it if the rules state you must reach the highest point. We can all decide for ourselves what feels right and for me, on Shipman Knotts I now do feel like I have reached the top.

The Mountain Camp

This is a great place for a camp and brings out the best Shipman Knotts has to offer. The ground is soft and comfy and the view across to the three great peaks of the Kentmere Horseshoe, Yoke, Ill Bell, and Froswick is sublime. Rainsborrow Crag, a 300-metre precipice on Yoke that drops vertically to the valley floor is particularly impressive. A short walk along the ridge in the direction of Harter Fell brings me to a small summit that isn't a Wainwright. Looking down above Snowcover Gill there is a great view down into Longsleddale and along Gatesgarth pass. Tarn Crags can be seen and the unusual structure on the summit.

Allen Crags - 784 metres
Southern Fells – 6th June

The Adventure – The Hulk

Despite the magnificent surroundings, there is something not clicking into place today. Seathwaite Fell looks amazing with the sunlight highlighting the steep crags. I can see the spot where I camped in the storm behind the largest of them. A huge white fluffy cloud hangs above the top and the sky behind is a dark blue. The grass is summer green and the oak tree at the base is in full leaf. My thoughts though are moving too fast. I feel very angry, everything is a bit rushed and even finding time to write some words for this book is a struggle. Inside my mind is a storm, swirling around and if I was anywhere else other than in my beloved mountains I would surely explode. The mountains have an effect that is calming, and soothing. The white waters of Sourmilk Gill running down between the side of Base Brown and the crags of Grey Knotts is a sight to enjoy. The timelessness of their existence contrasts with how I feel. In some way neutralising my anger. I love the mountains and it feels as if they love me too.

The Mountain Camp

Allen Crags stays hidden as I follow the deep-sided Ruddy Gill from Seathwaite. At the top of the gill, I can see Great End, it's Central Gully towering upwards. There are a few small tarns fifty metres down and west of the summit that would make great camping spots but today I've brought my bivvybag and plan to camp near the very top. There are great views all around. I can see the Langdale Pikes, the Scafell massif, and Great Gable. Arguably at its best angle on the other side of Sprinkling Tarn. With the sun setting behind and the light glaring off the water. Great Gable looks like a giant compared to its surroundings. I find a nice flat grassy edge to place my Bivvy and enjoy the view with a rock pillow made from volcaniclastic claystone. To make it a circular walk in the morning I follow the ridge over Looking Steads and Glaramara. Above a cloud inversion, the wind blows the clouds over the col with the sun rising behind. As they drift across it's a dreamy vision and the night's sleep on the mountain has made me feel a hundred times better.

Esk Pike - 885 metres
Southern Fells – 7th June

The Adventure – The Running Granny

I get to the van and then immediately must turn round and walk the same way as yesterday, all the way up to Ruddy Gill, taking in the view of Great End's Central Gully and to Esk Hause. Repeating the route makes me smile, a chance to enjoy what I missed out on yesterday. Today I'm wearing my running shoes as I am searching down the Running Granny. Angela White is aiming to run the Lakes 62 biggest mountains (those over 2500 feet) in 62 hours at the age of 62 and after bumping into her in early spring on Thornthwaite Crag I am going to say hello to support her. A kindred spirit having her own adventure in the mountains. When I reach Esk Pike she is heading up Bowfell so I run as fast as I can across Ore Gap. Named so because of haematite that gives the ground a reddish colour. It's a clear sunny day and thankfully I don't need to use my compass. Legend says it's not to be trusted. The path is uneven with hard stone slabs and large loose boulders. From the top of Bowfell I can see them at the Three Tarns and after a high-speed descent, I manage to track Angela down as she is climbing Crinkle Crags. We have a quick chat; she is determined to finish but may take a little longer than hoped. After saying goodbye, I turn and walk back rather more slowly to my camp over the best playground in the World.

The Mountain Camp

Esk Pike is a fantastic Bivvy spot, rocks abound so a tent is no use. With a bivvy, you can find a spot nestled between the grooves and notches in the crags to tuck yourself into. I love the simplicity of a Bivvy. First, I put down my matt on as flat a spot as I can find. Then I take out my Bivvybag which already has my sleeping bag inside, take off my shoes, and climb in. I use my rucksack as a pillow and that is all there is to it. Angle Tarn sits below to the northeast, and this makes a good tent pitch but you don't get the same view. From the summit of Esk Pike, I can see over Glaramara to the northern giants of Skiddaw and Blencathra with Derwent Water looking tiny in front.

Eel Crag (Crag Hill) - 838 metres
North Western Fells – 8th June

The Adventure – Mining

The highlight of the day is exploring Force Crag Mine. Originally a lead mine and later zinc and barytes it closed in 1991. On the way to Coledale Hause, I stop to investigate. There is still some accessibility for the determined in both the lower and the upper mines if you don't mind wet feet. I paddle through the green water and then moving a secret loose iron railing out of the way, squeeze between the remaining bars. It's like entering the Batcave and I can tell I'm not the first person to do so. This upper mine shaft is hidden around the corner from the old mine buildings, on the plateau above Low Force. They look as if they have been abandoned halfway through a shift. The mine goes into the mountain more than fifty meters underneath Hobcarton Crag. I'm stooped as I paddle through the water. I'm enjoying being inside for a change and my imagination dreams of finding a treasure chest. When I turn my torch off the blackness is solid. I continue as far as I can until a landslide blocks the end of the tunnel and I turn back empty-handed.

The Mountain Camp

The conditions on the summit are a lot different from inside the mine. The large flat top marked with a trig point is very exposed. The wind is blowing strongly, and the warmth is lost with its strength. Because the top is such a large flat area, I don't feel like I am in the high mountains, despite its height. In the wind, it is not easy to find a good spot to camp. At first, I try setting up my bivvy to use the shelter from the stone seat facing Skiddaw. The view is amazing however the wind is too strong. The good thing with a bivvy is it's easy to change your mind and move spots. I find a much more comfortable bed in the grass north of the summit above the crags which give this mountain its name. The view across to the ridge running to Causey Pike makes me look forward to taking the long way back in the morning.

Great Gable - 899 metres
Western Fells – 9th June

The Adventure – Wet Wet Wet

Great Gable is a great mountain although today it's not at its best. It is wet, cloudy, and raining. There is a strong wind blowing and it is hard work to get to the summit. I am very slow after three tiring nights in the bivvy. A damp clag hangs low over the valley. The path after Stockley Bridge up the side of Taylorgill Force has no view. I follow Styhead Gill along the awkward path. The large boulders feel uncomfortable for my feet. Twisting and bending to get good foot placement adds to the slowness. Huge cairns which on a clear day look ridiculously large are needed today. Waterproofs are only good up to a point, and that point has now been breached. I can feel my trousers cling to my legs and my collar is damp around my neck. The rucksack strap around my waste seems to open a door to let the water in. Plodding is what I'm doing now, no longer hiking. At the stretcher box on Styhead I start the final section of the climb. No one else is around, or at least in the mist, I haven't seen anyone else. The wind gets stronger and stronger on the way to the boulder field at the top. Visibility is only about ten metres and it's a struggle all the way. At least I don't have to walk back down today I think to myself. Finally, the summit plaque in memory of the Fell and Rock climbers who died in World War I tells me I've reached my destination.

The Mountain Camp

I reach the summit and amongst the stones and boulders and try to find a good spot. I can't. Ronald Turnbull told me on our Walla Crag camp about a hidden spot he'd found above Arrow Head Gully. It sounded perfect; a small shelf of grass big enough for a one-man tent with views over Wast Water. If the weather had been better, I would have tried to find it but not in these conditions. I want to get inside my tent and dry off a bit. I decide to pitch my tent just 10m east of the summit on stones that I lay flat. The tiny bits of grass don't allow the pegs to stick in very far, so I use rocks to hold them in place. Inside the tent everything is wet. I am uncomfortable and surprised at myself for remaining cheerful. Despite drying the inside as best I can it remains cold and damp. The tent shakes in the wind and this causes water drops to fall on me. I'm enjoying the challenge. The hiking is done and now I get to use my special talent, sleeping.

Grey Crag - 638 metres
Far Eastern Fells – 10th June

The Adventure – A Feast

It's dry when I park at the end of the country lane in Sadgill. An old couple pull up behind the van in a vintage Morgan convertible. I think they had better get the roof up quickly because rain is on its way. The farmer has a sense of humour and has a sign on his gate saying, 'Behind this wall is not a toilet.' I climb the stile, avoid the leftovers from people who can't read, and walk up the grass bank. At the next stile, I look back at Sadgill. It shines beautiful, green, and lush in the hissing rain. Reaching Great Howe, I am in the cloud, a couple on the way down tell me they've been in the cloud all day. Great Howe is a rocky spur and behind is a marsh crossing Stockdale Beck that I walk over before reaching Grey Crag itself. The wind blows my cap off and running after it I manage to grab it. There are no views from the summit, and I console myself with a great meal. My tea is a feast tonight, egg fried rice with ham, mushrooms, salami, tomatoes, olives and spices, chilli, and smokey. All fried up in the little porch area of the tent keeping me protected from the elements. Little treasures like this are a highlight of the day.

The Mountain Camp

Grey Crag is on the outskirts of the Lake District.
Looking east you can tell this is the edge and looking
west makes you wonder why you are here and not
there. I find a dried-up peat bog in a slightly small
hollow and pitch my tent. I can hear and feel the wind,
but this is the best shelter I can find. The ground is flat
and soft, and the pegs go in deep and strong so it's nice
and secure in the tent. The wind is doing its best to be a
nuisance, gusting and swirling from different directions.
Tarn Crag is the neighbouring mountain and to reach it
more marsh around Little Mosedale Beck must be
crossed. I'm not in the mood for a walk tonight and am
happy to stay in my tent.

Wansfell - 487 metres
Far Eastern Fells – 12th June

The Adventure - Annie

It's Annie's birthday. As much as I try and persuade
her, Annie doesn't like wild camping on top of a fell.
Annie, my daughter prefers campsites and animals. Last
night we stayed at Baysbrown Farm campsite in Chapel
Stile, like we do every year. It has myriad rope swings
(tarzies) above Great Langdale Beck that provide hours
of entertainment. Swinging in the sunshine and
dropping into the water with a splash is great fun. So is
the Via Ferrata at Honister Slate Mine. An iron way up
the side of Fleetwith Pike which was the afternoon's
entertainment. I'm sure one day I will be able to
persuade Annie to come wild camping. Maybe I should
have bought her a Bivvybag for her birthday. We
unsuccessfully try and find a lamb that wants to be
stroked and then it's time to drop her back home. The
sun is still out, and I head to the summit of Wansfell.
Time is of the essence; I want to reach the top to watch
the sunset. Parking on the Kirkstone Pass Road the
path leads down into squelchy bog and then follows the
stone wall upwards till the summit is reached. The view
east towards Troutbeck Tongue and the pretty
Froswick behind is great and looking west Coniston
Old Man and Wetherlam look fabulous.

The Mountain Camp

I pitch the tent up near the summit of Baystones with lovely views of Red Screes and Lake Windermere. There are lots of little grass flats in the undulations, looking as if they are designed as raised tent pitches. People would pay a fortune to camp here. It's very comfy and relaxing after a busy day. The peace and quiet of wild camping is one thing I will never tire of. Wansfell Pike which is part of the same ridge but with a different summit is often climbed from Ambleside. This way you go past the magnificent Stock Ghyll Force waterfall which although a tourist hotspot is very impressive. Tonight, though I'm staying away from there and enjoying having the summit to myself.

Lonscale Fell - 715 metres
Northern Fells – 13th June

The Adventure – Reflection

Sitting inside my tent overlooking Derwent Water, fantastic clouds sweep in and fade out while the sunlight highlights the mountains of Borrowdale behind. I think what have I learned so far on my camping adventure? The answers I come up with are.

Every Wainwright is fun to camp on.
It's lovely to have time to wander the fells
Life should not be a race against the clock
I'm pleased my adventure is noncompetitive
Filled pasta gets boring after 40 portions
Life is better when you relax and drift, forcing leads to frustration
If you cannot want for anything, you will be happy all the time.

I still have no answer to what I will do at the end of the year. I am not sure if I will be able to give up this way of life, and equally unsure if I can't, how I would be able to fund it for the longer term. It's not an expensive way to live but I still need to buy food and keep my van running.

The Mountain Camp

What makes Lonscale Fell special is its pointy little nose sticking out in viewpoint. This eastern edge of Skiddaw can be seen down Thirlmere valley from the top of Dunmail Raise. Unfortunately, this is not quite the top, nor is it the best camping spot. This is to be had on the other side of the summit where there are views over Keswick and Derwent Water nestled by the surrounding mountains. Following Glenderatarra Beck and then heading up through pathless terrain over steep grass between the crags makes for the most interesting way to the top. A much easier way is from Latrigg. Today I take a long route from the Blencathra visitor centre along the bridleway track past Skiddaw House as far as Whitewater Dash Falls. Then loop back over the top of Bakestall, Skiddaw, and Skiddaw Little Man, it's a great walk and way to traverse the biggest mountains in the Northern Fells.

Barf - 468 metres
North Western Fells – 14th June

The Adventure – The Bishop's Route

I walk up to the summit of Barf via the Bishop's white rock route. It is a steep scramble; hands are not needed in the sliding scree, but they are on a tricky outward leaning ledge. The rock is friable and creates a real sense of danger for good reason. The little mountain path winds its way steeply zigzagging up the route and along the vertical rock face, the views across Bassenthwaite Lake towards Skiddaw are as breath-taking as the view straight downwards. I am finding it great fun. It's not a scramble in the sense of Sharp Edge or anything like that, it's just a steep and tricky path with a high level of exposure. This may be what lulled the Bishop of Derry to drunkenly bet he could ride his horse to the top along this route. Legend says he tried, fell off, and died in 1783. He then died again in Italy 20 years later but don't let that spoil a good story. I'm enjoying this climb very much; the touch of the dirty rock, the smell of the pine trees, it is stimulating all my senses. A little bit of danger certainly helps one feel alive. A more recent legend, the Banksy of the Lakes has been at work a little higher than the bishop in the old ruins. Mysterious stone circles made from the slate have appeared and frame the view towards Borrowdale to the delight of all who find them.

The Mountain Camp

The wild camping spots on top are numerous and amazing. You can camp right next to the cliff edge with a vertical drop down to Bassenthwaite Lake and then have views up to the top of Skiddaw on the other side of the valley. The full Skiddaw family as Wainwright calls them can be seen, Ullock Pike all the way to Lonscale Fell and little Dodd in front. The scramble and then the cliff edge camp make it an amazing little mountain to camp on. It's fun to walk up past the Bishop but heading back down the route through the pine trees of Whinlatter next to Beckstones Gill is a safer and no less fun way.

Castle Crag - 290 metres
North Western Fells – 15th June

The Adventure - Time

I'm having a good time in the sunshine on Castle Crag. Crossing over Rosthwaite Steppingstones I follow the River Derwent to Pennybridge Dub. The water is clear and small fish can be seen in the stream. They, like me are not in a rush to get anywhere. At the weekend I witnessed a children's athletics race where time was the only important measure; one second up, two seconds down, three seconds faster, seven seconds slower. Children are taught to feel unworthy because of time. Always needing to be faster. Why is time so important and why is that a measure of success or failure? It shouldn't be and I think it leads to bad mental health. I'm pleased my adventure is not a race against the clock.
Castle Crag has been here for millions of years and a second. The second is not important and it will be here long after we have all gone. Mountains truly remind me of what is important in the world, and it's not seconds.

The Mountain Camp

I think about sleeping in the cave but decide it isn't for me. Milican Dalton lived in High Hows Quarry Cave during his summers and his epitaph 'Don't waste words, jump to conclusions' can still be seen scratched into the wall. It is a bit too large and exposed for me, the size of one of those humongous family tents. I prefer my caves small and compact like a wild camping tent. The best things come in small packages and Castle Crag is one of those. It's a little gem, fun to explore on all sides. I climbed it in the afternoon, passing ruins in the loose slate to the summit and sat in the sun for hours drinking Fizzy Earls on the sight of the old hill fort. Below me I watched sheep play hide and seek in the bright green bracken. Then I went back to the van for tea and now I am returning in the evening time. This time taking a scrambling route round the back, it is very steep, in fact, it might not be a route, it might be a fox path through High Hows Wood. It's fun and makes the Barf Bishop route seem easy, it doesn't have fallen trees to clamber above and below. I have a great view of Broadslack Gill coming down from High Spy. After completing the Castle Crag Girdle. I find a Bivvy spot on the now deserted top and finish a great day.

(Note: A Fizzy Earl is cold brewing a Lady Grey tea bag in a bottle of fizzy water.)

Branstree - 713 metres
Far Eastern Fells – 16th June

The Adventure – Sensory Deprivation

The view of Wood Howe Island is amazing as I drive to park at the end of Haweswater. It looks like it's from a different continent altogether, exotic and moody with mist hiding the hills behind and the island catching the light. The trees are full and green, and the water is low exposing a white outline of the island. It looks warm and tropical, it is deceptive. The reality when I step out of the van is a typical Lakes Day, damp and chilly. White cloud all the way means visibility is reduced to zero views in the mountains. It's a bit of a trudge hiking up Gatescarth Pass, although easy to follow it's not one of my favourite walks. I turn east at the top, cross over marshy ground surrounding Gatescarth Beck and follow the wire fence until I reach the large flat, only slightly domed plateau that is the top of Branstree.
I set my tent up behind the stone wall which runs down to Mosedale Beck and up to Tarn Crags. The wind is very strong, and it is the only place to get shelter. Inside my tent, I make a hot drink. Some days you get sunshine and great views other days you get no view and just white cloud. My wild camp on Branstree is one of those, I am finding it very refreshing, and a chance to concentrate on the inner rather than the outer view. I am discovering sensory deprivation can do wonders for your thinking and start to feel renewed, reinvigorated, and ready to go again.

The day has one final treat in store for me. When I leave the tent for an evening wander all the cloud has gone and the horizon glows orange in the setting sun.

The Mountain Camp

Branstree has a flat grassy top with endless camping spots although the views are limited by its expanse. If you want a great view of the west side of the Far Eastern Fells, then Artlecrag Pike which is west of the summit is the best place to camp. There is a classic beehive cairn on the subsidiary top that is worth a visit. It's hard to find a better-looking cairn anywhere in the Lake District.

Pavey Ark - 700 metres
Central Fells – 21st June

The Adventure – Ode to Herman Buhl

It's the summer solstice and climbing up Jack's Rake as the sun sets is as much fun as at any other time, my hands grab the hard rock and pull me up easily. Trying to find a suitable place to Bivvy for the night is however not as easy. Passing the famous tree after the steep scramble is a flat spot but this seems a little low down, so upwards I go. Next to the fallen chockstone that sticks up at an unusual angle is another little ledge. I try it but it is uncomfortable, so upwards I go again. The view over Stickle Tarn is magnificent and the drop perilous. Scrambling over a rock block after the slight dip in the thin track the perfect ledge appears. Just long enough for me to lie down with my feet dangling off the edge but feeling safe enough to sleep. This is an amazing place to Bivvy; absolutely brilliant and I don't think I will ever find as good a spot again. A hero of mine Herman Buhl is famous for his standing up Bivvy on a ledge descending from Nanga Parbat in the Himalayas. Prisoned by the dark he had no option but to wait till morning light. The sunrise was also my signal to leave and after reaching the top I climbed back down the Rake and to freedom.

The Mountain Camp

Pavey Ark is fantastic for its scramble and to sleep on it you must have experience and know what you are doing. In 2012 two people fell to their death from the Rake in separate incidents. If you are looking for a tent spot you won't find it on the scramble but there are plenty of places over the back of the summit in the grass next to small pools of water. The huge cliff overlooking Stickle Tarn is undoubtedly the best feature of this mountain. The tarn on a summer's day is a great place for a wild swim. Another great route to the top is via Easy Gully. It doesn't have the exposure of Jack's Rake but don't let the name fool you. There is one section when clambering is not enough, and a leap of faith is needed. Or a rope.

Haystacks - 597 metres
Western Fells – 22nd June

The Adventure - Tourists

This might be Wainwright's favourite, but it certainly isn't mine; there are people everywhere. They are here for a reason and that's because it is a beautiful mountain rising above even more lovely Buttermere but for me, they are a distraction. I walk past Gatesgarth Farm where they are setting up to film the latest Hollywood Blockbuster. Hundreds of vans with equipment and food getting ready for the star's arrival. I don't know who the star is, and I don't wait around to find out. Crossing over the mouth of Warnscale Beck running into Buttermere I follow the stone path upwards until I reach Scarth Gap. The route towards Haystacks although not as busy as Gatesgarth is too busy for me, so I change my mind. For the afternoon I walk over to High Crag. It's very steep zigzagging up the scree slope and my hard work is rewarded by the view down into Ennerdale Valley. The River Liza running down the middle and tall pine trees on either side are sublime. I head back to Haystacks at teatime when the crowds are thinning. The summit is a pair of rocky ridges with a small pool of water between them.

Sitting next to the cairn I think back to my days studying Geology. We went everywhere in a crowd then and it didn't seem to bother me. Hard hats and hammers at the ready. Was it just I hadn't discovered the pleasure of being on my own or did life's events shape me this way? Examining the rocks, it is the commonly found andesitic lavas on the surface, however, there is also a minor intrusion of the coarser microgranite running along the crest of the ridge.

The Mountain Camp

I visit Innominate Tarn, top up my water bottle and afterwards finally find the magnificence of this mountain. After climbing over a wire fence, I camp on the edge of the cliff high above Black Sail Hut. My view is from Green Gable, across Windy Gap to Great Gable and then I tick the mountains off in order, Kirk Fell, Pillar with Pillar Rock sticking up in front, Black Crag, Scoat Fell with Steeple in front, Haycock, Caw Fell and finally Crag Fell above Ennerdale Water and it is magnificent. With giant mountains behind me, on the side, and opposite across from a huge valley Haystacks is a great mountain after all. Now in the evening, I am alone on the mountain, and it makes it even better.

Green Gable - 801 metres
Western Fells – 23rd June

The Adventure - Key Concepts

Following Sour Milk Gill, I have my rucksack strap tied tight around my waist, in previous years it used to be a Tang Soo Do blackbelt. Courage, Concentration, Endurance, Honesty, and Humility are the five key concepts of this martial art. I enjoyed the sparring and struggled to remember the forms but what I loved most about it was the key concept philosophy. Undoubtedly, they have benefited me immensely on this adventure.

Courage - to spend nights on my own in the mountains. Whatever the weather, the pleasant and the freezing snow, gale-force winds or torrential rain.

Concentration- to not make any mistakes and injure myself or put myself at risk, to make sure I have all the kit I need for all circumstances.

Endurance - to keep hiking and camping night after night after night. Tiredness is not a reason to stop.

Honesty - to others about where and when I camp and to myself, I'm doing this adventure for me as a once in a lifetime event and I want to be able to look back on it knowing I gave it my best.

Humility - at times I have got excited by the attention and the fact I'm doing something that has never been done before, but Doro and my kids keep me in check and remind me I'm not special just lucky to have this chance.

What we are today is the sum total of our past experiences.

The Mountain Camp

Green Gable is a superior camping spot than its big brother. Location, accessibility, and terrain are all much better. Pitch on the grass with a view along the River Liza and down the valley to Ennerdale. I had hoped for a golden sunset, but the cloud has set it. My second chance is to look East for the sunrise in the morning and beautiful peach and rose stripes filled the morning sky. This is a terrific mountain and Windy Gap deserves a mention, it really lives up to its name. The col between Green and Great Gable funnels the wind and increases its strength exponentially. Looking the other way, a warm friendly feeling creeps over me when I realise, I can also see yesterday's camping spot on Haystacks.

Little Mell Fell - 505 metres
Eastern Fells – 24th June

The Adventure – Diamonds

It is a sunny day in the afternoon as I walk from The Hause between Pencilmill Beck and Lowthwaite Beck. It's warm and still, however, the clouds tell a different forecast. High in the sky and strung out in white wisps this means rain, as well as Doro, are due to arrive later. Wearing only crocs on my first visit to the trig point summit of Little Mell Fell, it takes less than 20 minutes. The ground is hard, grassy, and a ladder of brown earth footsteps makes the slope feel horizontal. This series of footsteps, where every hiker puts their feet in the same place eroding the sloping ground to a flat level is a charming sight. My second trip to the summit is with the tent, having decided it would be nice to have it set up before Doro and the rain get here. There won't be any more hikers visiting the summit today. I spend the early evening reading in the van until the rain arrives. It gets here before Doro, who turns up not long after. It's pouring down as we walk to the tent for my third climb up the mountain. Soaking wet we start the ritual of trying to get inside and take waterproofs off without soaking everything else. Wild camping is as much about rain as it is sunsets. Once we are delayered and inside the tent, it's nice and cosy, the patter of rain on the outside of the tent cocoons us inside. I tell Doro the drops of rain are her Diamonds. She smiles at me.

The Mountain Camp

Little Mell Fell is a small grassy hill and along with
Great Mell Fell they look different from the rest of the
mountains in the Lake District. Round and soft looking
I remember driving past this hill as a child always
wanting to climb to the top. It looked a lot more
appealing to me then than big and scary Blencathra did
on the other side of the road. The reason it looks
different is that it is made from sedimentary rock, the
Mell Fell Conglomerate. This is easier to erode and has
given it a soft appearance. There are lots of camping
spots on top and I think it would be great for young
teenagers on a first wild camp, away from adults as long
as they are taught the motto of leave no trace before
they camp.

Rossett Pike - 651 metres
Southern Fells – 25th June

The Adventure – A Low

The walk to the top of Rossett Pike is a lot longer than first appears. You can see the top about five minutes after passing Old Dungeon Gill, however, three hours later we are still not there. The path winds its way through the long-drawn-out valley of Mickleden and up the rockface in a very meandering way. My motivation is low today, and I am feeling very tired. Today marks a third of the way through my adventure. It's been raining and is a dull day with wind, it's not the sort of day that makes you want to head off into the mountains. Doro is doing her best to encourage me. One thing for sure is I won't make it to the end of the adventure if this feeling carries on. We stop to refill our water bottles from Rossett Gill and talk about bivvybagging. The advantage over a tent is it's lighter to carry and you can see the stars from your bed. The disadvantage is you can't see the stars if it's raining like today and you'll get wet. Doro remains to be convinced. Giving up never crosses my mind when I am on my own so why it does when I have company, I am not sure. We eventually reach the top and then the wind is even stronger as expected although at least the rain has stopped.

The Mountain Camp

Rossett Pike is a high bridge connecting the Southern and Central Fells. The top is a long ridge with three distinct summits and the highest is marked by a small cairn on the western side. We find a good camping spot sheltered from the wind on the flat grassy ground below the crags. Truly in the heart of the mountains. Bowfell looks massive rising up behind our camping pitch. Angle Tarn down below is a popular spot for wild camping but always seems dark and gloomy to me. We make walking back down to Langdale more interesting in the morning by leaving the path and following the stream, a tributary of Rossett Gill from the col directly downwards. There was a path here many moons ago and faint clues can still be seen.

Scafell Pike - 978 metres
Southern Fells – 26th June

The Adventure – Accident in the mountains

The sun is out and it's a lovely hot day as we follow the River Esk from the red phone box at Brotherilkeld Farm. Doro is excited, this is the big mountain that she has been looking forward to climbing. Heading for Great Moss the path is a winding delight and full of interest. Deep canyons and plunge pools abound. When we reach the great bog, we hear screams of 'help somebody, help, we need help'. Another walker is running towards us asking if we have any phone signal. We don't and neither does he. He tells us a man has fallen down Cam Spout Waterfall which is the direction we are heading. We reach the waterfall, and the man is lying unconscious on the floor. Two doctors, who by chance were hiking in the area are tending and have him in an emergency bag. Another man has the exact GPS on his Garmin. We take a photo of it and head up to Mickledore as fast as possible to get a signal. It's a long steep climb up the side of How Beck but we don't stop till we reach the top. Thirty minutes later the Mountain Rescue helicopter arrives. It does a fly-by to access the situation and then returns to drop off the volunteers who go to the man's rescue. I had started to think of the mountains as one giant playground but witnessing an event like this is a reminder that care is needed.

The Mountain Camp

The top of Scafell Pike is a rocky affair. Plenty of options for a Bivvy amongst the banana skins. The Nuttalls tell me they found a grassy spot on the summit to camp and eat their rehydrated custard powder from, although we couldn't see it, they are the guidebook writing experts. Wainwright recommends camping in Hollow Stones, but we took the advice of Ronald Turnbull (Mr T to his friends) and camped at Broad Crag Tarn. It has views of the gap at Mickledore and Broad Stand behind. A truly amazing wild camping spot, one of the best and deserted even on a Saturday night. In the morning it's a very relaxing place to be. The huge size of the mountains and the sunlight making the grass glow green puts everything in perspective. Doro has her legs sticking out of the tent, breathing in the fresh air and drinking tea while I make breakfast outside on the stove. It's a great end to her weekend in the mountains. 'I feel like I am in a fairy tale, on another world', she says.

Steel Fell - 553 metres
Central Fells – 27th June

The Adventure – Sausages and Bob Graham

I shouldn't have eaten a train of six sausages that had gone moldy before setting off up Steel Fell from Dunmail Raise. Cooking by the roadside I mistakenly thought a good cremation of the sausages would suffice. They were Cumberland sausages, and I'd been looking forward to them all weekend as they marinaded in the van's heat while I was away camping. It's a very steep climb up Steel Fell from this side and by the time I got to the top the sausages were coming out my bottom, fast and in liquid form. It's not what you want to happen when sleeping in a bivvybag Thankfully the sausage train passed fast through the station, and I was ok half an hour later.

Feeling much better I fall asleep in my bivvybag as it gets dark. Not long after I am disturbed by four runners doing the Bob Graham Round. I can hear them approaching with their head torches on. 'What's that over there?' says one of them.

'It's a blue bag,' says another.

'Oh, there is a man in the bag,' says the third.

'I hope we didn't disturb you?' finishes the fourth, as they all shine their lights in my direction to examine the man in the blue bag. With four spotlights shining on me, I think to myself; yes, you did disturb me. How would you like someone walking into your bedroom in the middle of the night and shining a torch in your face? But I reply 'No it's ok. You're looking fresh, enjoy your run.' And off they go.

The Mountain Camp

The top of Steel Fell may appear to have two summits, Steel Fell is the easterly summit while Dead Pike is the name given to the westerly. There are plenty of nice places for a bivvy or camp on Steel Feel with a couple of overgrown tarns also occupying the summit. In the morning I need my head net to keep away the midges before getting up and checking out a great and often missed view north of the summit. The path from Dunmail reaches the plateau and heads to the top but heading in the other direction there are amazing views over Thirlmere towards Lonscale Fell with its pointy nose and Blencathra.

Blencathra - 868 metres
Northern Fells – 28th June

The Adventure – Lazy Day

It is a gloriously hot day on Blencathra, 25°C. The sun is out with very little wind, and I get an early start wanting to make the most of the day. I don't get very far before I stop for a snooze in the long grass looking towards Skiddaw. This sets the tone for the day, short potter uphill, stop relax, make a brew, and then repeat. If there was a record for the longest time it takes to get to the top of Blencathra then I've probably set it today, over five hours from the Blencathra visitor centre to the highest of six tops, Hallsfell. On a sunny day like this, there is no rush. Time in the mountains is what I love and today time seems infinite.

I sit and have my lunch looking down the fantastic Halls Fell Ridge, it is a great steep route to the top along a narrow rocky ridge with vertical drops on either side. A friendly man comes over for a chat, he tells me he has climbed to the top via Sharp Edge which is an even more exposed ridge.

I tell him I am camping on all the 214 Wainwrights; he looks at me like I am strange and moves on. I spend the afternoon taking photos near the summit puddle and then get a surprise from Hebz, an Instagrammer. She has climbed Sharp Edge with her boyfriend and come to say hello. No one has ever asked to have a selfie with me before and I'm a little surprised as well as flattered. At least not everyone thinks I am weird for all my camping. After the goodbyes, I think if everyone else is climbing Sharp Edge today so am I, alone on the ridge it makes a fantastic evening's entertainment under a red sky.

The Mountain Camp

Blencathra has six summits but is definitely one mountain. The ridges are separated by five streams, viz: Blease Gill, Gate Gill, Doddick Gill, Scaley Beck, and Scales Beck all of which flow into the River Glenderamackin. Walking along the long top and looking down into the gullies and streams is a great way to enjoy being up high on the mountains and makes the most of the effort needed to climb it.

For some reason, unknown to me, Blencathra always has loads of insects. If I could have chosen a season to camp on it midwinter would've been preferable but the yellow bag gets what it wants. As I look for a place to Bivvy from the countless great options on the summit the midges are everywhere, as well as thousands of birds eating the midges, I wish they would hurry up and get them all eaten.

Glaramara - 783 metres
Southern Fells - 5th July

The Adventure – Hidden Paths

I take an unusual route up Glaramara, turning left two
fields after Seathwaite at Hind Gill, and head for a
weakness in the cliff.

I start walking up the track and it is steep, no, actually it
is very steep and it's not a track just a faint trodding of
grass. An expert bushman would have trouble following
this trail. I'm no expert bushman and losing the track I
traverse south across Hind Side. A strange gate in a wall
opens out onto a cliff. I look down but decide not to
pass through and fall to the depths, so turn back and
look upwards. Before reaching Red Beck there is a gully
leading up towards Looking Steads.

The track is very steep and hard work. No, actually it is
very very steep and because it's very very steep it's very
hard. Any steeper and a rope would be needed.

And because it is very very steep and very hard it is
EXCELLENT because nobody walks this way, and I
don't see anyone from the car park to the summit. My
heart is pounding in my chest, a mixture of nerves and
exertion. This is hard, scary work, and the rucksack as
always is like an anchor pulling me down.

If only all mountains had hidden paths like this, you
know what? Most of the big ones do.

The Mountain Camp

A myriad of crags and dips and grass patches and streams abound on the summit plateau. There are 5 summit Nuttall's on this one mountain such is the length of the ridge. I find a great spot with views of Great End and Gable but there are so many great spots how do I know I have found the best? I don't; so, I better come back another time and try them all until I know for certain. Combe Gill on the northern slopes is a magnificent example of a hanging valley. There are plenty of tarns on the summit and I make a note to myself that this is definitely one to return to after the adventure has finished. Maybe next time I'll come with just a bivvybag.

Great Dodd – 857 meters
Eastern Fells – 6th July

The Adventure - Greatness

Great Dodd is very high up, 850m so it's surprising that at the top it's just a grassy dome with no more interest than Little Mell Fell. It might be called the greatest Dodd, but I can't see why.

It's good, it's a Wainwright so of course it is, don't get me wrong, but great?

Watson Dodd has better views, Rest Dodd is aloof and charming, Hartsop Dodd is always amusing as it's Pasture Bottom. Even plain old Dodd is full of interest with its trees and trails.

So, what makes Great Dodd great? With a lack of other attributes, it must be its height. Well then, if you can be great just by being tall then I like the sound of that.

(Note: the author is 6'4" tall, although does not consider himself great)

The Mountain Camp

A great big grassy dome with very little shelter, if there is no wind then it's a great spot. I've been up here countless times and not yet experienced no wind, so what you will get is a windy grassy pitch with nice views. As a camping spot, it is just that, nice. Its normally visited along the great ridge from Helvellyn to Clough Head however to make it an individual summit today I start from Dowthwaitehead. I follow the Old Coach Road before turning up and around the back of High Brow making it a quieter route, the only other activity is a farmer loading sheep onto his lorry with the help of a very clever Collie. Walking up from the eastern side the going is a good grass path that never gets too steep. A more exciting way to the top is following Mill Gill from Legburnthwaite on the western side. This is a scrambler's route up the stream but is not suitable if you have a tent strapped to your back. The summit has a stone cairn, and the flattest piece of grass is to the east. It is lovely being high on the mountains in the summer warmth, as the sun sets over Skiddaw the benefit of the mountain's height is revealed, a view of tangerine and orange fills the sky. In this moment this is a great place to be.

High Hartsop Dodd - 519 metres
Eastern Fells – 7th July

The Adventure – All Time High

Today is a high, happiness seems to have seeped into my bones. Summer is approaching, plans are afoot for some Bivvybagging camps with family and friends and the weather is glorious. It's the sort of day that fills your childhood memories. Sun everywhere you look. effortless movement with no aches and a golden haze hovering over the bright green mountainsides. Above the blue sky is cloudless and whitewater hisses over grey rocks and falls down the side of the fell. Sitting beside Dovedale Beck the smell of summer is in the air and the taste of a warm orange lingers long after it has been swallowed. I'm looping over Dove Crag to reach High Hartsop Dodd and steep crags guard the way to the Priest Hole. I can't help but visit to explore but wish I hadn't. Dirty and full of litter it's a victim of its popularity. Looking down over Hogget Gill I can see the ridge whose end is known as High Hartsop Dodd before it drops steeply down to Sykeside. This is a day when there are views in every direction. I savour them all as I make my way slowly over the tops. The tops of the mountains are what I like most, much better than their bottoms.

The Mountain Camp

High Hartsop Dodd is a little 'un and also a great 'un for a wild camp. Steep on both sides down to Kirkstone Pass and Hogget Gill. I perch my camp right on the top looking over Brothers Water and straight at Angletarn Pikes and Place Fell. The ridge behind rises up towards Little Hart Crag and camping here feels like setting your tent up on the end of a diving board. There are steep drops on three sides but a gradual incline on the fourth. This is another day I have spent entirely on my own and I like it. Without other people, the world is a much less stressful place. I'm sure lots of others must feel the same and I wonder if they do, why don't they escape to the mountains as I have.

Sallows - 516 metres
Far Eastern Fells – 8th July

The Adventure – Be the Change

A sallow can be either a type of willow tree or a moth. I wonder if I will see either today. Then I wonder if I did see either, how would I know, as I know not what the specifics of either look like. Then I wonder if I might see both together, a moth emerging from its cocoon hanging from a willow tree and capture it in an amazing picture. Then I stop wondering and start wandering, something I am much better at. This is Camp 78. The number is nothing special on its own, neither is camping on Sallows. Anyone can do this anytime.
But as Aristotle said 'the whole is greater than the sum of its parts and this is just another steppingstone on my journey to being the first person to sleep on all the Wainwright mountains. In the future will this be known as The Dawn of Mountain Sleep Bagging? Only time will tell, in my dreams, it inspires others, hopefully, it's a good story to tell and if nothing else it is a lot of fun for me. 'You must be the change you want to see in the world' This is my way of showing others how to live a better life and take a step away from the world I was caught up in before. If everyone took a step away, then we could make a real change.

The Mountain Camp

Sallows is on the extremities of the Lake District. Normally reached by hiking from Dubbs Road it makes a very pleasant camping spot. Grass and heather occupy most of the summit plateau. There is a large bed of shale that emerges on the very top which is a fitting crown for this hill. The view north towards Yoke is the highlight. This is not an exciting wild camp but a relaxing one. The pine trees at Garburn Nook add a bit of contrast to the surroundings and act as an indicator for when to leave Garburn Pass to head up the slope. If you just visit the summit for a minute to bag the Wainwright before hiking off to Sour Howes, then you are not really doing it justice. Mountain Sleep Bagging gives you time in the mountains, time that you could spend in a thousand different ways, but none would be as rewarding.

Arthur's Pike - 532 metres
Far Eastern Fells – 13th July

The Adventure – Against the Clock

Arthur's Pike may be only 532 m high but when you've
got 300 miles to drive to get there it's a long way.
Limping along the M6 in third gear at 40mph I'm not
sure I'm going to make it today; the clock is ticking. I
have a lot of camping to fit in this year and need my
trusted companion, Base Van Camp to get me to the
start of today's climb.
The day started under a rain cloud with a burst tire on
the M1. A delay for the breakdown truck and then two
new tires were needed at the garage. After lunch in
Chesterfield, my van was fixed and I'm on my way. But
only briefly. Thirty minutes of driving through the Peak
District and I must stop again. This time the lights on
the dashboard and oil spraying from the bonnet mean
there is another problem, and the engine control unit
won't let the van use 4th or 5th gears. The breakdown
man tells me it is not going to get any worse so
travelling at tractor speed I continue for over 200 miles.
Thirteen hours since I set off, I am finally turning off
the M6 and heading for Pooley Bridge with just one
hour of daylight left.

The Mountain Camp

I don't think there is anywhere in the country that for a one-hour walk can provide such amazing views. Arthur's Pike may not be the tallest mountain but its positioning midway along Ullswater makes it an ideal viewpoint to watch a sunset behind Great and Little Mell Fell. And what a sunset it is today. Parking at the mouth of Swarth Beck I head upstream before zigzagging through Auterstone Wood. Rather than heading to the Barton Park crossroads, I head straight up through the bracken. It's fully grown now and seems determined to cling to my ankles as I try and get a move on. With the corner cut off I follow the mud and stone path to the summit and then find a small ledge to pitch my tent. I could have flown to anywhere in America with the length of time it took me to get here today, but the view wouldn't have been as good as this.

Gibson Knott – 422 metres
Central Fells – 14th July

My Adventure - Speed

The best way up Gibson Knott according to Wainwright, and I agree is via Green Burn. Gibson Knott is spectacular for wild camping. Full of little ledges just big enough for your tent and I take my time getting to the summit. I enjoy a snooze near the waterfall of Green Burn until it is broken by the noise of the flying Typhoon. As normal the first is too fast to spot but my eyes are tuned in to see the second. There are over 500 of these planes in existence and they practice their low-level flying skills over the mountains of the Lake District at speeds over 1000 miles per hour. Rather them than me, as I like to enjoy my time in the mountains. For me, the enjoyment comes from the slow pace and the perspective that the mountains will still be here long after we are gone. This makes me feel calm. And I like feeling calm. Competition increases speed and that is what I like about my wild camping adventure, neither speed nor competition is a factor. In a world where everything from running times to global warming is speeding up, having time in the mountains to get away from that, relax and understand there is a different way to live your life is priceless.

The Mountain Camp

Solitude is what you find on Gibson Knott; and bracken this time of year in July, plenty of bracken. And a stream flowing all the way up making gurgling sounds. And at the top? More solitude. Who wants to be on top of Gibson Knott when so near on the other side of Bracken Hause is Helm Crag with its Howitzer and all around in other directions are mountains you have heard of? Well you do, because you can have this one all to yourself. There are a couple of cairned knolls on the summit ridge with the westerly being considered the top. The rock is volcaniclastic siltstone and a much comfier camping spot is on one of the grass ledges looking down over the valley Far Easedale Gill with Easedale Tarn and Blea Rigg behind.

Outerside - 568 metres
North Western Fells – 15th July

The Adventure – Ghyll Scrambling

Summer is here, it's a scorcher today. Looking at the world through sunglasses always increases my focus on the mountains. I can't explain why but they seem much clearer. The coconut smell of my sun cream adds to the holiday vibe. I'm walking from Braithwaite underneath Barrow between shoulder-high vibrant green bracken fronds on a dry dusty mud path heading for Stoneycroft Ghyll. The ghyll is a classic for adventure. Laminated mudstone and siltstone rock has been worn smooth by the water and forms natural chutes and slides. There are places to plunge off and in weather like this, it would be great fun. I've got a pack on my back so settle for walking up the stream and avoiding the deepest plunges. In the still sections of the ghyll, the surface water has been warmed by the sun. Damselflies with their metallic blue bodies and delicate wings skim around the surface. On the lower part of the stream, I have to avoid groups with hard hats and wetsuits scrambling over the rocks. They look curiously at a man with a cap and rucksack heading the other way but are too busy flinging themselves off the top of waterfalls to say anything. Once I pass between Causey Pike and Stile End the stream is less dramatic although I have it to myself. The water is shallower here and I follow as far as I can before heading onto dry land for the final part of the climb.

The Mountain Camp

Stoneycroft Ghyll leads almost from the bottom to the top of Outerside. What a way to climb a mountain by following the stream to its full height. The pointy summit of Outerside is in view all the way up the ghyll, sitting up high waiting patiently for your arrival. The only flat spot for camping is at the very top. The best view is looking out over to Skiddaw and the surrounding fells of the Coldedale Horseshoe give a closed-in feel to the other directions. It is not easy to find a good camping spot and I make do with pitching on top of the heather and looking down into Force Crag mine.

Dodd - 502 metres
Northern Fells – 16th July

My Adventure – Hammocks

Wild camping in the summer often means a warm
sunny day is spent relaxing waiting for the evening hike.
Today is one of those days. Pottering about the North
Western Fells in the day I arrive at Millbeck in the early
evening. Hiking through Dodd Wood at this time is
peaceful. The only noise is coming from me and
cracking a branch underfoot I disturb an Osprey, it
takes flight, and its large wingspan does well to fit
through the pine branches. Some tree felling has taken
place on the lower slopes under the shadow of Carlside.
There is a caravan in the middle of the clearing, but it is
deserted. Higher up the air is still warm and smells like
the Mediterranean with the scent of pine. Through the
gaps in the trees, I can see Bassenthwaite Lake and Barf
on the other side. The summit has a stone pillar but not
the right trees for a hammock camp. It takes a bit of
time searching for the right trees and eventually I find
the perfect spot following the south path from the
summit to the subsidiary peak. A pair of perfect
conifers are standing resplendent, four metres apart
from each other. The angle means I can string my
hammock up with the sun setting behind me and a
perfect view over Keswick and Derwent Water.

The Mountain Camp

Dodd, just Dodd. This Dodd doesn't need a first name. Like a famous pop star or Brazilian footballer, one name is all it needs. You might think hammock camping is all about being hidden in a deep dark wood but here is an exception. Dodd offers an exceptional wild hammock camping opportunity. This is the only Wainwright you can hammock camp on the summit and although hammocks are not my preferred way to sleep this opportunity could not be missed. It would be an equally good Bivvy spot but not suitable for a tent.

Hammock tips: bring extra rope so you can reach the trees. At this time of year, a midge head net is also handy. They are best for back sleepers, if you sleep on your side or front, they are not as comfy. But still make great photos.

Causey Pike - 637 metres
North Western Fells – 17th July

The Adventure – Ghyll Scrambling II

Today I get to do what I didn't manage two days ago. The weather is just a perfect, hot sweltering sun and no breeze. It's the start of the school holidays and my kids, Will and Annie have joined me for a day's ghyll scrambling in Stoneycroft Ghyll. This time I have a crowd to show off to and plunging from waterfalls is given meaning. The water is clear and light-coloured rocks can be seen underneath. We walk up the stream avoiding the deep plunges but scouting them out for our descent. The highlight looks to be a jump into a narrow steep-sided gorge that requires the use of a metal chain to haul ourselves out with afterwards. Up the ghyll we go, all the while Causey Pike is looking down on me from above. Reminding me that when the Bivettes go home at the end of the day my work is still not finished. When we reach the top of the waterfalls we turn around and slide our way down in screams of excitement.

Exhausted is not too strong a word to describe how I feel by the time we reach the bottom, after several extensions to repeat the best sections, the goodbyes are said and I start a slow hike up to Rowling End. I pass along Sleet Hause, before making the final climb up the little rocky scramble. At the top, fuelled by the desire to rest, I set my tent up. I am rewarded with a comfy night protected from the wind on a soft soil mattress and sleep like a log.

The Mountain Camp

Five crinkles, it could be Crinkle Pike but it's not: it's Causey. Mirroring the mighty Crinkle Crags but in a North Western Fell way. You know what I mean. A bit softer, a bit easier, a bit smaller, a bit more grass. Causey even has its own little scramble to the top but even that is less than the Bad Step.

But there is a saying less is more and for good reason because Causey is a magnificent mountain. It looks beautiful from afar and up close, it is just as lovely. A choice of four dips between the knuckles to pitch your tent and views all around.

Sale Fell – 359 metres
North Western Fells – 22nd July

The Adventure - Illusions

33° is the temperature and in the afternoon, I have a snooze in the van with the doors open parked under the shade of Fisher Wood. It's so peaceful and all this camping is taking its toll, when I get the chance for extra rest, I take it. I can hear a babbling sound from Wythop Beck but no other sounds. I find it very easy to drift off while I read about Wainwright's great illusion and await Doro's arrival this evening. If you stand in a certain spot on Sale Fell there is an illusion that makes it look like it joins onto Skiddaw and Bassenthwaite Lake does not exist, it's a trick of geometry. Due to the angle of the land, Wythop Wood on Sale Fell appears to merge seamlessly into Dodd Wood on the other side of Bassenthwaite. No view of the lake is visible and to the uninitiated, it would be a surprise to find a lake down there. Wainwright must've really liked this illusion because he wrote three pages on it in his book and a total of 12 pages on Sale Fell. That's two more pages than he gave the much more visited Cat Bells.

The Mountain Camp

There is something very famous five about Sale Fell, different routes up from different sides of the small hill where all parties could meet at the top, illusions making it seem like it is attached to a much bigger mountain and a hidden lake, a huge king lake that is hidden in plain sight. It is a marvellous fell, full of glory with countless spots for a night's camp and perfect for youngsters. I may not be a youngster anymore, but I feel like one when Doro is around. We sleep with just the tent mesh above us as we don't need the flysheet and falling asleep, we see countless stars and the full moon rising. The moon is bright orange, a blood moon. Once risen it lights the landscape at the expense of the stars almost a brightly as the sun. In the morning it is replaced by the real sun which reflects over the water in the distance. It is a beautiful way to start the day.

Kirk Fell – 802 metres
Western Fells – 23rd July

The Adventure - Magnificence

We start from Ennerdale Water, and it is a long walk along the River Liza to the foot of Kirk Fell, about 7 or 8 miles. The light is clear, an artist's dream in the magnificent hot summer sunshine. The huge pine trees and the piles of chopped down logs at the side of the path stand out like 3D objects, which obviously they are but they seem to gain an extra realness in the light. Much more alive than last time I walked along here in the drizzle. Following the forest track, we crunch through pine forest and the scent mixing with the heat makes it feel like we are in a foreign landscape.

Did I say a long walk? I meant an enormous walk; it feels like 70 or 80 miles in the now not so magnificent midday sun. My rucksack is heavier than normal and by the time I reach the foot of Kirk Fell, 5 hours later having had a lunchtime swim with Doro in a plunge pool I am in the Black Spot, all hope is gone. 'Leave me here, this could be my final resting place.' I say, 'I am frazzled.'

The relentless sun, the 30-degree heat, and the view of the near-vertical final climb all seem too much. Magnificence now seems to be just a point of view.

But great rewards don't come easy and after resting by the river we head up Black Sail Pass, thinking it should be called Black Spot Pass because I'm starting to feel much better now. By the time I reach the final exciting scramble to the summit of Kirk Fell I am thoroughly enjoying myself.

The Mountain Camp

Kirk Fell is a big mountain but because its brothers are even bigger it looks small. What happened to the top of Kirk Fell? It's like a soft-boiled egg that has had it's top chopped off to get to the good stuff.

Wild campers should be thankful for this, as whilst the top of Great Gable and Scafell Pike are stony battlegrounds, Kirk Fells summit provides comfy grass to pitch your tent, stony bluffs to shelter from the wind and a tarn for liquid refreshment. Not to mention the views, those views of endless mountains. After following the old fence posts to the summit, we find a great spot for a camp with a view of Pillar and the sun setting behind leaving the sky a brilliant orange to match the colour of the tent.

Pillar – 892 metres
Western Fells – 24th July

The Adventure – Bikini in the Mountains

Today is an occasion when the yellow bag doesn't get
to decide my mountain, Doro does. We wake on Kirk
Fell and are having an all-time high. It is so much fun
living on top of the mountains that we don't want to
come down. It's a beautiful slow start to the day. We
drink earl grey tea with honey and milk while watching
the sunrise turn the sky orange high above the depths
of the Liza valley which are hidden under cloud. The
tops of the cloud shimmer as they catch the light. Kirk
Fell will now forever feel like an orange mountain to
me. We drop back down to Black Sail Pass and then
start the climb up to Pillar prior to stopping by the
small tarn for lunch. Doro has brought her bikini for
sunbathing. I've never seen such beauty exposed in the
mountains before, neither I think had the hiker who
passed while commenting 'beautiful views.' I assume he
was talking about Great Gable.

The Mountain Camp

A huge lump of rock, gargantuan. Not pointy or domed but just massive. Certainly not a pillar shape more like a spoonful of mash potato shape, make that three spoonfuls.

There are two tarns on the way up from Black Sail. The top one is better and would make a lovely wild camping spot if you weren't a summit camper. But why wouldn't you be, carry some water with you and at the top the craggy view from the champagne cork of Gable stretching to Scafell is something worth celebrating. This is the view that we go for albeit a better one for the sunset colours is to camp above Pillar Rock looking out over Ennerdale Water. That said looking towards Scafell Pike you don't get the colours of the sky, but you do get to watch the colour of the rocks change as the sun sets. It makes a beautiful change, like watching the hardening of stone. Once again, we pitch the tent without needing the flysheet and with time pressing make an early descent down High Beck and through the Ling Mell plantation early in the morning.

Barrow – 455 metres
North Western Fells – 25th July

The Adventure – Keep making decisions

This is a popular fell so for camping you want to get there late. I arrive at sunset and try all four directions out with my bivvy; indecision is the killer. To avoid this it's important to keep making decisions. Neither Base Van Camp, Yellow Bag nor Doro are here to help so I choose to face Skiddaw and look forward to seeing the sunrise in the morning. Vowing to be back at least three more times to try out all the other options. The key to happiness is having something to do, something to look forward to and someone to share it with. Tonight, I have two of the three ingredients for happiness. Now all I need to do before next time is to persuade Doro to try sleeping in a bivvybag. Doro tells me she is keen to have a go one night but as with most first-timers, it's a step into the unknown. Bivvybagging will have to wait though because the next time she visits we have planned to hike the Bob Graham round. A shared love of the fells is one thing fell runners and wild campers have in common, but the biggest difference is highlighted by Bob's quote 'if you spend a minute on the top of each summit to admire the view that's an extra 42 minutes to your time,' whereas I like to say 'if you spend the night sleeping in the mountain that's an extra 214 days to admire the view.'

The Mountain Camp

The problem with Barrow, and it's quite an important one; is where do you place your Bivvy? Do you want to watch the sunset behind Grisedale Pike? Do you want to look at the marvellous sweep of the Coledale Horseshoe? Do you want to look out across Derwent water to see the Helvellyn skyline? Or do you want to face the mighty Skiddaw? If only all tough decisions in life were such fun to make. The grassy hill has a stony top made from mudstone and looks down into Stoneycroft Ghyll on one side and Barrow Gill on the other. As it gets dark, I am snuggled in my Bivvy when a couple come past completing the Coledale Horseshoe and say a passing hello. It's not the first time I feel like someone has entered my bedroom unannounced, but of course they have as much right to be there as I do. All this time in the mountains has started to make me feel like a guardian.

Mungrisdale Common – 633 metres
Northern Fells – 26th July

The Adventure – Thirsty work

After a week of driving with three gears, my van is in for repairs and so I have no Base Camp. A selection of Northern Fells have been put into a red bag and I walk from Keswick to Threlkeld along the old railway line. It has been reopened as a tourist attraction and follows the River Greta. The tree shade along the cycle path is dappled and plenty of sun is getting through although a coolness can also be felt rising up from the river. The trees and grasses at the side are a full assortment of different greens, light, dark and emerald. The best route up Blencathra is via Hall's Fell Ridge. It's the quickest route to the top and leaving the trees behind I head up the laminated siltstone ridge. Some of the rock is worn smooth and to make the most of the ridge I commit to following the highest part all the way up. Its thirsty work and easier side paths are available but following the crest all the way adds extra entertainment to the climb. The ridge drops steeply down to Gate Gill and Doddick Gill on either side. Looking up I can see the only escape is to reach the top. Once on the other side of Blencathra it has none of the exciting scrambles and dropping down to Mungrisdale Common I pitch my tent near the summit.

It's been dry for days and my evening's entertainment is searching for water, Roughton Gill is dried up at its source. I am following it downstream but not having any luck finding water. I have a change of plan and follow the Herdwicks that look well-watered and find a spring on the common. They know more than they let on do sheep.

The Mountain Camp

Why is this a Wainwright? Asks everyone who hasn't spent the night there. Those that have, know why. Featureless and flat it is but what it lacks in kerb appeal it makes up for in location. Sandwiched between Skiddaw and Blencathra like the pearl in an oyster shell. Mungrisdale Common has a unique beauty and charm and is the perfect spot to get away from it all. I'm lucky we are in the midst of a summer dry spell and the ground is not its usual bog today. I've positioned my tent in the grass which is straw-coloured towards Lonscale Fell and have a great evening relaxing after a long day's hike.

Meal Fell - 550 metres
Northern Fells – 27th July

The Adventure – Predator in the Bracken

This is the time of year when the bracken is in full growth, it looks lovely, tall and vibrant green. The fronds are all uncurled and palm-like. The thick coverage on the top of the plant leaves space underneath where the stalks grow. They are great for making dens and you might think it's the perfect place to go to the toilet in privacy while in the mountains. Hidden in plain sight you can go about your ablutions unnoticed. However, be warned! A predator lies lurking in the bracken with a bite more tenacious than a great white shark, only smaller. The predator seeks out heat like a guided missile and there is nothing Ticks like more than a warm bottom to bite. Pull your pants down in the bracken at your peril. I've learnt this the hard way after my trip through the Barrow bracken. Once they bite, they don't like letting go and removing three of them was not a pleasurable task. Today I walk past the bracken, thankfully not needing the loo. I'm not going to make that mistake again.

The Mountain Camp

Imagine a horseshoe of mountains and then stick a random mountain in the middle, well that mountain is Meal Fell. The reason is Trusmadoor, a remarkable pass. A deep cut into the landscape, steep on both sides and not like any other pass in Lakeland, is a Geographer's delight.

I find a great camping spot on the northern prow of Meal Fell. Below the summit, the ground drops away and then turns upwards for a final wave before dropping down to farmland. The lip is flat enough for my hooped bivvy and the views make it feel like I am camped on the end of the earth in the most glorious camping spot. Binsey is visible behind Over Water and in the hazy setting sun looks a lot more impressive than you expect from its 316 metres, punching well above its weight. It reaches up against a backdrop of the Solway Firth and its twin summits look like the eye sockets on a crab's back.

Helm Crag - 405 metres
Central Fells – 28th July

The Adventure – Celebrity Chef

It's a rainy day, it's been raining all day and I'm sure it will be raining all night but for the hour that is tea, it has miraculously stopped. After 90 wild camps, I have my best evening meal yet. Harrison Ward, a celebrity mountain chef who has cooked with Mary Berry is climbing Helm Crag to cook my dinner. Harrison turned his life around after being overweight and drinking too much. He seems a genuine guy wanting to spread his message of a better life through his love for the fells and cooking outdoors for others. Tonight, he cooks red pepper and mascarpone gnocchi on his triangular stove he has carried up the mountain. After adding the sauce, he knocks the pot over. The gnocchi falls onto the sheep mown grass of the summit. I'm not fussy and it still tastes delicious, going very well with the good conversation. Who doesn't love talking about being outdoors in the mountains? Although I'm not sure Mary would have been quite so keen to pick the gnocchi off the floor before eating it. Harrison isn't camping so he heads back down the mountain as the rain and darkness fall. In the morning I unzip my tent and look out into the drizzle wondering what time he will be back to cook my breakfast. He never shows.

The Mountain Camp

Helm Crag looks fantastic, and its summit crags are unmistakable when viewed from Grasmere. The lion and the lamb or the cannon? That is the question of where to place your tent. There are lots of places to pitch up between the crags that don't just give you shelter but also, and unusually enhance the view. Before deciding I go searching for the ditch after the secondary summit ridge as described by Wainwright. It sounds like it will make the perfect camping spot in this weather, protected from the wind and the rain. But on discovering it the sides are too steep and the bottom too pointy for a camping spot. I also discover a small cave nearby. Big enough to crawl into but not comfortably. I settle on the cannon or howitzer and have the perfect view of it from my tent door.

Bowscale Fell - 702 metres
Northern Fells – 29th July

The Adventure - Acceptance

Mungrisdale village is not common, it's quite posh. I park my van next to the River Glendermackin so I can dip my air bed to fix a puncture. I feel like a dirty tramp, which essentially is what I have become. I can't wait to get up the mountain where I leave my tramp status behind and become king of the mountain sleep baggers. King only in name because as there are no other mountain sleep baggers, I have no one to rule over, but a king in a kingdom of one is still a king. What I notice when climbing up and up is not the struggle or the steepness but during my frequent rests, I notice Great Mell Fell. I realise what an important fell it is. Although I have only spent 1 night there, I have spent countless days looking at it and recognising it. More so than even Scafell Pike because what Great Mell Fell is, is a standalone mountain. I see myself in this fell. Alone and proud, noticed but distant.

To be content you need to know yourself and accept what you are. It's not an easy journey but once complete your mind will be at rest.

The summer has and is becoming busy with camping companions and today is a chance to be on my own and enjoy the mountains for myself without distraction. I have been so distracted with the camping and the sunshine and living in the present, high all the time in the mountains, I've only just realised this is what I have wanted. I have finally found happiness.

The Mountain Camp

Bowscale Fell is a huge grass monster with arms and legs going off in different directions and a tongue sticking out. It also has a Tarn nestled in the heart of the beast as if it was well er… a heart. From the summit the smooth back of Blencathra can be seen and down onto Mungrisedale Common. The tarn named after the mountain is no longer visited by Victorian ponies and makes a great wild swimming destination. I try and set my Bivvy up in the summit shelter, but it is not a very good shelter, and the wind gets in. It's blowing strongly today so I drop down a bit and end up bivvying on the path looking out towards the Pennines. This is the flattest bit of ground I can find, and I fall asleep under an orange glow.

Kidsty Pike - 780 metres
Far Eastern Fells – 3rd August

The Adventure – Gambus Puree III – Summer Camp

Gambus Purée III joins me today for his summer camp. Leaving Mardale we walk via Long Stile in glorious evening sunshine. The summer's drought is in evidence as are the towns ruins sticking above the surface of Haweswater. With Blea Water down on our left and Riggindale with Hugh's Cave on our right, it's a brilliant ridge to climb and leads to the summit of High Street. We are in good spirits after going sub 20 on a run this morning, although having done so doesn't make the walking any easier. Time ticks on and we are racing the setting sun, hoping to get to the top before it disappears. A myriad of good Bivvy spots presents themselves along the way, but we are summit campers and must reach our destination. It doesn't disappoint being the best of all we have seen. We throw down our bags right on the rocky arete and prepare our tea. Food improves in flavour the higher you go, and we eat a tea of instant mash and lardons. Soul food in the mountains. The nighttime brings a clear starry sky with a crescent moon. We try to see past the labels of the constellations and understand what is actually there, balls of fire, burning hydrogen giving off light that takes thousands of years to reach us. We are looking at the past. In the morning we have an uninterrupted view of Earth's own red fireball sun rising way below us over Nan Bield Pass and giving the mountains a golden layered appearance, it is fabulous.

The Mountain Camp

Kidsty Pike has a prominent peak but there is no domed back, no Kidsty Fell. Or well maybe there is but it's called Rampsgill Head and has separate Wainwright status. However, this mountain doesn't need a body to be great, just a nose will do. I like a prominent nose. We find a brilliant daredevil Bivvy spot on the summit, a little shelf directly above the steep drop over the vertical crags. The spot is only big enough for one.

'Would you like to sleep their Gambus?' I say.

'Really? On this cliff?' says Gambus peering over the edge down into the depths of Riggindale.

'Yes, this is where England's last golden eagle used to live, I'm sure it would have sat there looking down at the mice of Riggindale'.

'But I don't fly.'

'You don't eat mice either but don't let that stop you.' And being the kind father I am, I let Gambus sleep there while I find a flat level grassy spot on the Western side of the peak.

Carrock Fell - 663 metres
Northern Fells – 5th August

The Adventure – Old School Friends

The Iron Age fort is long gone, destroyed by the Romans. But the summit of Carrock Fell still resembles a place of occupation. Today it is occupied by me, and an old school friend not seen for 30 years, Quinny, or to give him his adult name, Mike. Despite having visited the tops of all the Wainwrights and running the Bob Graham round under 24 hours he has never been wild camping. Jumping straight in at the deep end tonight is his first Bivvy. We cycled around the Lake District as 15-year-olds and despite losing touch have maintained very similar interests, although different memories. I remember climbing a hill in the evening but not which one and Mike remembers going down Kirkstone Pass on a bike with no brakes. After the BBC news piece, he got in touch, and I'm pleased to say it wasn't to return the black eye I gave him one day at school. A sudden outburst while fighting over a history book which when he reminds me, I have no real explanation for. I tell him 'What makes a Bivvy the best of all wild camps is the fact you are fully outside; your head is in the open. When you wake in the night you see the stars, lots of them given you are on a mountain top. And when the sunrises you see that too, without even having to get up.'
'You sound like an advert, do you put the matt inside your bag?' Mike asks
'All the advice says you do but personally I don't like to. It makes me feel to squashed and I can't roll around.'

He ignores my anti-advice, puts his matt inside his bag and wakes every hour during the night.

The Mountain Camp

Carrock Fell makes an unusual camp because you look away from the mountains of the Lakes and towards the Pennines, over flat green fields of the Eden Valley towards the long great stretch of raised land. Camping here you get to see the sunrise and it has soft grass and moss to Bivvy on rather than a pile of fort stone rubble. The morning can't come soon enough for Mike and although he is glad to have done it once, I'm not sure he will be using his bivvybag again. Well, you can't win them all.

Skiddaw - 931 metres
Northern Fells – 7th August

The Adventure – Bob Graham Round Night 1

Doro has always wanted an adventure and she is joining me for her summer holiday. Our plan is to walk the Bob Graham round and camp on Wainwrights that I haven't yet slept on. I watch a glorious sunset while waiting for Doro to arrive. It's late when we start from Moot Hall at 10.30 pm, and it's raining. As we climb up in the darkness the rain gets heavier and after we pass Jenkins Hill the wind kicks in; Strongly. The summer's drought is definitely over, and we struggle to make ourselves heard by each other. The rain is blown into our hoods and then drips down soaking our underlayers. We have head torches on but with the dark and the rain, it's hard to see much more than two metres in front of us. The headwind is pressing our clothes tight against our bodies. I recognise the sculpture on Skiddaw Little Man which means we took the long route, but it matters not, we carry on. No path is distinguishable in the dark and rain. All stones look alike and after getting a bit too close to Broad End cliff above Tongues Beck we use a compass bearing to head for the col between Skiddaw and Little Man. At 2 am we find a flat spot just below the summit plateau and struggle to put the pole-less tent up in the wind. Water is everywhere and we climb into the tent soaking wet.

The rain drips off our waterproofs and inside the tent is as wet as outside. 'If we get the sleeping bags out now, they are just going to get soaking wet,' I say, 'maybe we should sleep in our clothes?'

'Ok,' replies Doro, and exhausted we cuddle together on one air bed in our dripping clothes and spend the night freezing, waiting for daylight to save us from this torture. The tent does its best to protect us from the wind but every time a strong gust blows water drops from the roof. We haven't yet even climbed the first of 42 mountains on this round.

The Mountain Camp

Skiddaw is the Giant of the North. A great mountain of mountain size proportions. It looks big and heavy, and it is also windy, strong winds are often found on the summit. There must be something about it that attracts the wind, but I am no meteorologist. The summit is long with several shelters that could pass as a Bivvy spot for the desperate but are no good for a tent. Flat grass for a tent is hard to find which explains an absence of wild campers except for dedicated Mountain Sleep Baggers.

Watson's Dodd - 789 metres
Eastern Fells – 8th August

The Adventure – Bob Graham Round Night 2

We start today soaking wet underneath the top of Skiddaw in cloud, pleased to be packing the tent away and getting some good hiking under our belts. Fell runners will try and run the Bob Graham round in less than 24 hours but we're going to take five nights camping and enjoy the views along the way. Well, that was the plan however it's now afternoon and as we head up Clough Head constant rain and cloud are all we have seen so far, 'what mountains are over there?' asks Doro

'I haven't the foggiest, it's a mist-ery to me,' is my not particularly funny joke but is the best I can do in these conditions. It's answered with raised eyebrows and a sigh, we walk in silence for a while. There is only so much you can talk about when in every direction it's white and your clothes are damp and uncomfortable. If there is nothing good to say, then best say nothing at all. After we pass over Great Dodd things start to brighten up a bit, our spirits and the weather. By the time we have set up our tent, the sun has broken through the clouds. Still full of moisture they hang low, as if too heavy to float. Huge, white puffy clouds appearing beached on the ground unable to get into the sky, like a balloon without enough air.

We are above them and the view is spectacular. For the twenty minutes it lasts, the warm rays of sunlight soothe and relax our tired bodies. The sun also energises the clouds, and they start to lift and fill the sky. It's a great way to end the day and tonight we have the luxury of a sleeping mat and bag each.

The Mountain Camp

The view from the summit of Watson Dodd is my favourite in all of Lakeland. I fell in love with it on my first Bob Graham round, tired with sore feet and a desire to stop it refilled my joy pot and kept me going. Looking west the ground drops steeply away between Mill Gill and Stannah Gill. Legburthwaite at the bottom emphasised the height and on the other side of Thirlmere, I saw layers of golden mountains behind Bleaberry Fell. On that day turning to look south I got the best view of a wide ridge that goes on and on and on. Today it is not visible, maybe that's a good thing. Knowing that we still must climb all those mountains might be too much after the day we have had. Rest is what we need and the ground on the summit is soft grass and very flat, it makes an ideal camping spot.

Sergeant Man - 730 metres
Central Fells – 9th August

The Adventure – Bob Graham Round Night 3

It's a very wet day, after waking up on Watson's Dodd we walk past Helvellyn. 'This weather is wild,' Doro says.
'I'm sure it will stop at some point.'
'What did you say?'
'I'm sure it will….'
'It's the wind, I can't hear you.'
'I said, I'M SURE IT WILL.'
'Will what?'
'STOP'.
We head down to Grisedale Tarn, we couldn't be wetter if we swam across, but we don't. We go up and down Fairfield, then over Seat Sandle.
'The weather will just do what it wants.' Doro's live in the moment attitude means the length of times it's been raining doesn't matter to her.
'Well, it must stop at some point, it's been raining for three days now'. I'm getting a little fed up of it.
'What did you say?'
The words don't reach, carried away in the wind. I shake my head and think about abandoning at Dunmail Raise. My dad, who is on support crew duties meets us with hot tea and coffee. We sit inside his car, on towels to catch the dripping and discuss the situation.
'You are doing well,' says my dad. He is always overly positive. He had been waiting five hours in his car for us.

'It hasn't stopped raining once this whole time'. I whine, ignoring the nice twenty minutes on Watson's Dodd.

'But it's good fun,' says Doro

I know then there is no way I will be getting let off her adventure and resign myself to the arduous climb up Steel Fell. What's the point of this? I think to myself as the rain falls down even heavier. Then I realise, I am actually enjoying myself, out here in the elements. We've not seen any other hikers all day even though it is August. It feels like we can accomplish anything if we can keep going in this weather and I can't think of any place or anything else I would rather be doing. We consider camping on Calf Crag but decide to press on to Sergeant Man as there is still some daylight left. We don't want to spend longer than necessary in the wet tent.

The Mountain Camp

Sergeant Man's summit is reached by passing over bogs and then following a path up next to Mere Beck waterfall. There are a few good spaces sheltered in the crags, nice and flat and very romantic. A perfect hideaway. We find a brilliant camp next to the waterfall, fitting for a day that's been constantly wet. The tent just fits in between the pools of water, and I have to stand in the puddle to secure the guys. You can only get wet once, and that happened a long time ago now. Inside the tent, we have a hot drink of tea to warm us up. I strip off so I'm naked in my sleeping bag, knowing tomorrow I will have to put my wet clothes on again. We don't rush to wake up.

Scafell - 964 metres
Southern Fells – 10th August

The Adventure – Bob Graham Round Night 4

Rain makes you wet, and it also makes you heavy.
When you're carrying a heavy pack and then you give it
a good soaking for four Lakeland days, everything in
your pack is double its original weight. The tent is
soaking wet, and all that water is now stuffed into the
bottom of my rucksack. Doro isn't concerned about
that, it's me that carries the tent. What she is concerned
about is the big mountains. Today is the day she has
been looking forward to most of all. We tick off the
Langdale summits in quick fashion and then reach
Bowfell. Lost in the mist we lose the Bob Graham
shortcut and find ourselves halfway up a dangerous
cliff. 'I don't think this is the way'. I stop for a second.
'It looks like it just gets steeper up there, and these
rocks are coming loose'
'Maybe we should go back down'. Doro pauses.
'That's easier said than done'. I try and peer through the
mist, but the rain keeps coming and I can't see anything
other than the drop.
We try and backup; the rocks are slippery, and it is heart
pounding time. One slip now would send us back to
Rossett Gill.
'I think I can see a way out'. Finally, we reach the
Climbers Traverse and make our way to the summit.
A long day surrounded by white cloud and rain
continues. We are feeling more tired all the time, and
this leads us to make another silly mistake on Broad
Crag. 'Is this where we left the rucksacks?'

'I think so, but I can't see them'. I can't see anything for that matter. Thick clag is hanging around and our decision to leave the bags near the main path while we ticked off the summit now seems a daft idea.

'I think it is this way we climbed up from'. Doro says pointing in what seems to be a random direction.

'Are you sure? we left them near the big boulder, I thought the bright yellow and red rain covers would make them easy to find but I can't see anything in this cloud'.

'There are lots of big boulders.'

'Yes, I realise that'. I've already camped on Scafell Pike and time is pressing. The white clouds are starting to turn grey as the day draws to a close and we need to reach Scafell for the night's camp. The rain isn't stopping and it's all getting a bit too much of an adventure. We regroup our thoughts and follow the main path south to Broad Crag Col. The bags haven't turned up and we then must retrace our steps north,

'There they are,' I cheerfully point at the rucksacks east of Broad Crag. The zigzag from Ill Crag is very confusing in the mist.

'That's where I said they were,' exclaims Doro.

The Mountain Camp

Scafell has lots of great routes to the top, but the rocky summit isn't suited to wild camping. Foxes Tarn however is a delicate little spot, big enough for one tent or a Bivvy and it feels great, like a safe haven tucked away in the middle of the massive mountains. But don't expect sunshine. If you're lucky enough for it to be shining, then the steep walls on all sides will most likely block it out. That's not a problem we are faced with today. The route up to Foxes Tarn is a steep gully with high walls on either side and to make it harder it has been turned into a waterfall by all the rain. Water is pouring over the rocks and spraying up where our hands and feet make contact. It's been very hard going in the weather, all our clothes have been soaked, and we are absolutely drenched. Exhausted we pitch the tent next to the tarn which is overflowing due to the rain. We are still smiling. Life is not about waiting for the storm to pass; it's about learning to camp in the rain.

Red Pike – 826 metres
Western Fells – 11th August

The Adventure – Bob Graham Round Night 5

Today will be an easy day as I need to roll a two and land on Red Pike, no point rolling a five or six and then landing on a Wainwright I have already sleep bagged. The cloud persists on the top of Scafell and it's a long walk down. At Wasdale Head the sun comes out and we stop for an ice cream. For a moment it feels like a summer holiday. Then we look at the walk up to Yewbarrow and wish it was still hidden in cloud. The steep path goes straight up and looks as hard as it will be.

'Stop a minute Doro, have a look at the view,' is an excuse for a breather as we reach the heather line.

'Look over there, you can see where we came from. That's Scafell Pike and Scafell and the gap is?'

'Oh wow, Mickledore, Aww'. Doro really likes Mickledore, it brings her happy memories of our time camping at Broad Crag Tarn.

After a slow-paced relaxing day, we approach the top of Red Pike as a thin mist rolls in. The breeze is quite strong and after a clear afternoon the mist appears as if being poured into the valley. It thickens and thins and fills up the valley of Mosedale below. Standing on the cliff edge above Black Beck we look down as the low setting sun shines behind us. 'Oh, wow, what's that? Can you see? It's like a rainbow'. Doro points out. 'And look, it's my shadow inside. It's waving back at me. Oh Wow.' She is as giddy as a three-year-old with the excitement.

'Cool, it's a brocken spectre'. My excitement matches hers, and I join in the waving. We look down over the cliff as the sun shines and frantically wave as fast as we can. Waving back are two angel versions of ourselves as if we had fallen off the cliff and then floated back up. 'Welcome to the exclusive mountaineers club.' I tell Doro. 'It's your reward for spending so much time in the mountains.'

The Mountain Camp

Red Pike is a rocky climb, we find it pleasant to scramble up the andesitic lavas and before the cloud had a nice view of Kirk Fell, Doro's favourite mountain. Wast Water looks particularly dramatic in the setting sun. A clinical clean line separates steep scree and water.
The top is grassy on one side and doesn't exist at all on the other, as Mosedale Crags drop infinitely downwards. We decide to camp on the grassy side and just manage to get into the tent before the rain starts again.

Bob Graham Round – The Finish – 12th August

Heavy cloud greets us in the morning and rain and wind. This is what we are used to by now, it wouldn't seem right finishing in the sunshine. Steeple can't be seen from Scoat Fell but we know it is there and head down through the thick clag to reach it before retracing our steps, passing Pillar and summiting Kirk Fell. 'I'm sure it's this way,' I say on the top compass in hand. We are looking for the descent route, but as we can't see more than five metres it's confusing on the figure of eight summit. Doro doesn't answer, knowing it's best just to let me get on with it. After Great Gable we must cross Windy Gap. 'Wow. It's so strong'. Doro links my arm, and we are crouching low to battle the wind. 'Whoaaah, hold on'. A gust pushes us, and we shuffle more than a few feet sideways. 'Keep moving when the wind relaxes and hold on in the gusts.' We take my advice and slowly reach the top of Green Gable. Wet and tired we keep plodding on. The plan is for a final night camp on Hindscarth before finishing in the morning. My Dad, the support crew meets us at Honister Pass. 'You two came down there fast', he is referring to our descent from Grey Knotts. It didn't feel fast but after he repeats it for the third time we just agree. His help has been vital to us and refreshed we make the steep climb up Dale Head and reach Hindscarth. A wide-open mountain top greets us. The wind is howling, and water is dripping from our gloved fingertips. We can see the lights of Keswick over ten miles away in the distance and darkness descends.

The wind is pushing us around and we sit in the shelter and try to make a hot drink in the rain. We have been on the move for over 14 hours today having and its decision time. 'Shall we try and pitch the tent or just head for the finish?' I turn to put my head above the shelter and try to look for a place to pitch on the summit. As soon my face is above the wall it is smashed into by the wind with such force I must duck back down. I feel like a soldier trying to look out of the trenches. Doro tries and is met with the same punch from the wind. We look into each other's eyes and know the answer, we can't camp here tonight it's not safe. It's a long walk back, we climb Robinson and despite our tired state still enjoy the tricky descent to Scope Beck. The road back to Moot Hall via Stair follows, it's raining all the way and we finish in a deserted town, an hour over five days after we started. Doro's answer says it all when I ask her how she feels? 'Like I've had the best adventure of my life'.

Souther Fell - 522 metres
Northern Fells – 13th August

The Adventure - Rest

The day after finishing the Bob Graham round walking
up another mountain is taking as much mental energy
as physical. We leave the van next to the River
Glendermackin at Mungrisdale and zigzag around Low
Beckside. There is still some wind around and light
drizzle in the air but the downpours from the last five
days seemed to finish at the same time we did.
'Nice to see you mountains, how have you been?'
'Very well thank you, you're back soon?'
'Well, you know me I love a wild camp, can't get
enough'. Went the imaginary conversation in my head.
When the ghost army walked passed and told me to
stop talking to the mountains, I knew I needed a big
rest. I explain to Doro that on a Midsummers Day in
the sixteenth century Southern Fell was the sight of a
mysterious illusion. An army cavalry was seen marching
across the summit all day long and verified by sober
witnesses, yet no trace of them was ever seen again.
This was the original Leave no Trace which all wild
campers should abide by.

The Mountain Camp

Is Souther Fell part of Blencathra or its own mountain? It doesn't really matter because it's a beauty. The long thin top means it is easy to imagine a Spectral Army marching across it and the col at Mousethwaite joins it with Blencathra. The River Glenderamackin circles the fell completely. Dropping down one side of the col and acting like a moat around a castle The Grand Old Duke of York would have loved this hill, all the troops marching up and down and being a freeman of the city so do I. The reason is because it's a great comfy camping spot with a fabulous view of Blencathra's saddle. We find a sheltered spot on a downslope from the summit and set up camp. It's Doro's last day of her summer holidays and after watching the stormy clouds turn to dark, we sleep a deserved deep rest well into the morning.

Sour Howes - 483 meters
Far Eastern Fells – 14th August

The Adventure - 100

When the wind blows some people build walls others build windmills. The wind is certainly blowing today. I have my old favourite tent, so am ready for anything. I leave my van at Dubs Road and head for Sour Howes. It's my 100th camp tonight and I feel proud of getting this far. I'm back on my own and feel like myself again. It's a strange existence being human, we are pack animals but when I am around others I feel as if I am not myself. Only when I am on my own do I feel like me. Freed from the need to please, wait for others or meet their expectations, I feel like I can finally relax. I walk through Beckstone Barrow, the grassy knoll is a vibrant green, long lush grass from the summer's growth. Relaxed is how I feel. I am not even halfway yet in my camping adventure and the end is nowhere in sight. I don't want it to end so that is a good thing.

The Mountain Camp

Sour Howes is mainly grass and hummocks, charmingly accessible yet still tricky enough to feel like a challenge. The top is an amazing place for a camp with views of the Troutbeck Tongue horseshoe in one direction and the full length of Lake Windermere in the other. There are countless places to camp in between the hummocks, which look like a set of sand dunes that have turned to grass. I decide that as I have my storm tent with me, I will opt for a view rather than shelter tonight. The ground is comfy to sleep on and once fully pegged out my tent can withstand any wind. It may not be a windmill, but I don't feel the need to hide behind a wall either. Being exposed to nature is I suppose, the biggest attraction of wild camping. There is a connection between us and the elements. A fundamental understanding within our bones that this is what we are. We are not a machine, designed to be inside, processing countless bits of information. We are flesh and bone and meant to be outside in the world. Even when you are outside in harsh conditions and having a challenging time, you still enjoy it afterwards. This is in stark contrast to all the times you find achieving your desires in the modern world leaves you with only a hollow feeling afterwards.

Clough Head - 726 metres
Eastern Fells – 20th August

The Adventure – Fright in the Night

Alex Staniforth, the endurance athlete, and charity founder is attempting the Bob Graham round solo, unsupported and in under 24 hours. He is due to run past Clough Head summit at 11 pm.

It's raining when I set off in the afternoon from Threlkeld or more accurately drizzling, but it isn't dampening my mischievous spirit. I leave the tarmac and follow Birkett Beck, cross over the Old Coach Road and climb the steep path for the second time in a week. I set my tent up next to the summit shelter and have about three hours to wait, it's still drizzling. I pass the time in my tent as it's getting dark outside. The red dot of Alex's tracker is getting nearer, he is at Blencathra. It's time for me to leave my tent and set my trap to scare him. This is just what all new wild campers fear might happen to them in the middle of the night, but it never does. Only to endurance athletes running with a tracker. Putting a light on in my tent and a full-beam on the cairn to create a dark space, I hide behind the trig in the shadows and wait. I can see his red dot climbing up the steep hill and then see his torchlight through the mist and rain. The breeze is blowing strongly, and the rain is moving sideways. As he approaches, I crouch into the set position. When he reaches the trig, I take a deep breath and jump out shouting AAARRGGGHH …………

The Mountain Camp

I rather like Clough Head, the steep one. Such a noticeable mountain, yet unless you're a fan of the Wainwrights you might not know its name as you drive past it on your holiday to Keswick. Maybe if it was called Great End, you would remember the name, but Clough Head easily slips the mind. However, once you have climbed to the top it will be the steepness that you remember. The reward once you get there is it feels like downhill all the way to Helvellyn, along the greatest flat ridge in all of Lakeland. If climbing the steep path is not for you then a more exciting route is via Fisher's Wife's Rake through steep crags. Legend has it that Fisher was a shepherd, and he made his wife bring his lunch up to him every day through this route. For wild camping, the highlight is the full view of Blencathra and all its ridges.

Angletarn Pikes - 565 metres
Far Eastern Fells – 21st August

The Adventure – Beauty to be Shared

Well, Angletarn Pikes had to come out of the bag at some point, but on a Saturday, in August, I expect it to be busier than Glastonbury. Am I annoyed? Yes, but I put my annoyance on a moving cloud and let it float away with the wind. Mindfulness has taught me this and Doro has taught me mindfulness. The reason it is busy though is because it is beautiful. We hike up the ever-steepening slope to Boredale Hause and then up to the summit. I look down and am reminded that beauty should be shared. I am glad Doro is here to see it with me, back for another week's holiday. Maybe that is why Yellow Bag chose it for us today, so we could share the beauty. 'Oh, wow,' says Doro, 'It's so pretty'. The tarn even in the rain that is now pouring is a magnificent sight. We rush to get the tent up and once again don't quite manage to do so before we are soaking wet. The misty clouds blow over and it's a very atmospheric camp. We discuss bivvybagging and if we ever get a sunny day, we might give it a go.

The Mountain Camp

The tarn is the number one destination for all new wild campers and why wouldn't it be. For less than 90 minutes' walk, even with a heavy pack you can be in the mountains, sitting next to glistening water with enticing islands and looking at views of Striding Edge in the distance. It will take several visits before you have tried all the pitches around the tarn and can decide which is your favourite. Angletarn Pikes has two summits and lots of bog between them. The best camping is with a view of the tarn. Tonight, we are not camping at the water's edge but just below the summit on a grassy ledge which is probably the best spot of all. Brock Crags comes in and out of view on the other side of the water and it's a dreamy sight.

Steel Knotts - 432 metres
Far Eastern Fells – 22nd August

The Adventure – When morning comes

It is nearing the end of the summer season and the weather is already heading into Autumn. I have a few nights to spare as I am aiming to be on 107 camps at the end of the month. This will be halfway in terms of both seasons and camps to spread my adventure evenly throughout the year. Maybe then I should have waited a day before camping, but here I am in the rain and wind again. Doro is with me, and we are cocooned in our tent as night falls. The spoken word, created by our laughter, vanishes in the passing air. Who says the Lakes is busy in August? There is no one to eavesdrop here.

In the morning we are rewarded for the effort made last night. Waking up on the mountain top all the hard climbing work has already been done. We emerge from our cocoon in the fresh morning air. Below and all around our lofty perch is a blanket of cloud leaving us marooned on a summit island. 'Oh, wow,' says Doro not for the first time. There are countless wonders to look upon when you go wild camping and cloud inversions are one of the best. The sun is above us and with the clouds below there is nothing to stop it from reaching us, the warm heat of the early sunrise means we are in no rush to head down. It looks like we could just step out onto the thick cloud and walk to Place Fell as if marching across unbroken fresh snow. We don't try it.

The Mountain Camp

Steel Knotts is a raise on the ridge running up to Wether Hill. Pikeawassa is the name of the summit, it's a sharp rock outcrop. This fine pinnacle gives the mountain a significance it would lack without it. Next to it is a flat piece of land just big enough for a tent, gardened by sheep they have kept the grass nice and short. There are steep drops away from this point on all four sides which gives the feeling that our tent is on a castle turret. It's a great place for a wild camp, far better than the popular Hallin Fell which sits opposite.

Dove Crag - 792 metres
Eastern Fells – 23rd August

The Adventure – Saying Hello

We park at Low Wood in the sunshine, walk between Wood Side and Brothers Water and follow Dovedale Beck upstream. It's a hot day, maybe we are not used to this and that's why we are having a difference of opinion. 'Why do look at everyone?' says Doro
'It's what I do, I prefer having the mountain to myself but if there is someone we are passing, I feel I should say hello'. Doro likes having the mountain to ourselves even more than me.
'They're just people, you are never going to see them again, you can just let them walk past'. Our discussion on what you should do fills up the entirety of our walk to the summit. The same activity can be viewed differently depending on how you are feeling. If you feel good all is well and enjoyable and if you feel bad then everything is a problem, filled with frustration. In the end, we never agree on the correct solution. It is a good job the view is nice. 'This is more like it,' I say as I cook tea outside the tent while Doro is inside protected from the plagues of flying ants that have awoken with the sun. 'Yes,' she says 'No one else is around now. It's just us on the mountain top'. We watch the sunset behind Great Rigg which because of its size blocks out all other views. 'If it's this weather tomorrow, shall we Bivvybag?
'That sounds like a great idea'.

The Mountain Camp

When wild camping on Dove Crag the big question is should you plan to sleep in the Priest Hole or not? If you do, get there early, and defend your turf. Suggestions to other potential cave dwellers such as 'there is a good spot down there near the sheep shelter' or 'a couple of guys had a great Bivvy next to the waterfall' increase your chances of having it to yourself. As does generally being an unpleasant person so that nobody would want to share it with you. Discarded beer cans, smoking, litter all help create this image. It all sounded a bit too much hard work for us. We decided a summit camp on the western side with a view of the sunset would be a much better option.

The Knott - 739 metres
Far Eastern Fells – 24th August

The Adventure – Mrs Bivvy

Today is the day Doro becomes Mrs Bivvy. If all goes to plan by the morning, she will earn the right to use the name. It will be her first Bivvy night and we set off from Hartsop full of excitement. The excitement is soon replaced by puffing and panting as we make our way along the stone track, past Hayeswater and up the steep grass zig zags. At the summit, the sun comes out and we know it will be worth it. We had been hoping to watch a spectacular sunset and up until then, the clouds had been spoiling the fun. It's windy on top so we get in our bags early and eat our tea. After tea, warm in her bag the future Mrs Bivvy doesn't want to get out again, so I take her in my arms and carry her from one spot to another searching for the ideal camp. We find an amazing spot to watch the sunset from. On a flat grass ledge west of the summit, we perch on the edge and the ground below us drops steeply down to Hayeswater. More carrying is needed as it gets dark and we shuffle back for more protection and sleep until the sun comes up on the other side. In the morning, still lying in our bags surrounded by damp grass and misty still air I ask, 'So Mrs Bivvy, what did you think of Bivvybagging?' 'It was very enjoyable and relaxing to watch the sky', she has a little giggle and looks intently at me with her loving green eyes 'to be able to watch the sky until you fall asleep'. Her eyes and her smile say it all, she loved it and will be back for more.

The Mountain Camp

The Knott is a perfect dome separated from the walking path and standing proud looking down on the hamlet of Hartsop. The sides slope down in all directions, to the east towards the path and on the west down to Hayeswater. This slope is broken by a flat ledge ideal for a bivvy or a tent. Perched on the edge looking across the abyss to Gray Crag and further afield to Grisedale Hause the layers of mountains rise on either side. This is one of the very best camps to watch the sunset from. The ground on the ledge is thick grass and comfy and it's big enough to camp on the edge or further back to avoid any wind coming up Pasture Bottom.

Arnison Crag - 433 metres
Eastern Fells – 25th August

The Adventure – Relative Mountain Theory

Climbing from Patterdale the going is tough today.
There is a dry heat, and the air is dusty. We were feeling
tired after last night's Bivvy and queuing on our
lunchtime trip up and down the Helvellyn scrambles
used the last of our energy. At least Arnison Crag is
deserted as we leave Grisedale Beck and make our way
through the bracken. A stone wall follows the ridge and
there is an insect hum in the mountains tonight. The
noise of summer rings in my ears. Arnison Crag is only
just over 400 metres high. Too tired for talking I am left
with my thoughts. However small a mountain appears
on paper when you are at the bottom and moving
slowly the top is always a journey away. Relative
mountain theory I call it, all mountains have the same
sequence of feelings from bottom to top. Relief at
setting off, the false promise of an easy climb,
realisation it is hard work, head down determination to
get on with it, the expectancy of hope, is that the
summit? and weariness when it isn't. Finally, pride
when you are on the top. I experience all these feelings
before finally reaching the summit then forgetting
about all the hard work and setting up camp.

The Mountain Camp

Arnison Crag's summit is split in two by a huge notch, the slightly higher side has the cairn, but the other is nearer Ullswater and is perfect for a camp with amazing views. Goldril Beck and Rooking Gill can be seen joining before flowing into the lake and in the other direction is Birks, looking down over Arnison like a big brother. Great photo opportunities abound, and we stand on the higher summit and try to capture the perfect wild camping dream picture, one man and his tent on the lower summit framed with Ullswater in the background. Sadly, it's too late in the day and the sun is not playing. It is playing though, in the morning, we open the tent flap and see a beautiful lake, lit up and glistening like a postcard.

Hopegill Head - 770 metres
North Western Fells

The Adventure – Halfway

Today's camp is my halfway point in what I have called my Sleeping with Wainwright adventure. The Wainwrights are the mountains, and the name refers to sleeping on the mountains, anyone thinking anything else about the name is revealing a lot about themselves. Spring and Summer seasons have been great, an all time high. I've still got the harder two seasons, Autumn and Winter to go but after 107 great camps in all weathers, I am still wanting more. 'It's your day Bivvy,' says Doro. 'We can do what you want to do'.
'Thanks, I'm not ready to go inside the tent yet. Let's wander a bit more'. We have been watching the sunset for the last few hours, a fruit salad sunset, sweet purple, and orange colours have filled the sky. Now they are fading, and the moon is lighting up the mountains. We can see in the dark without the need for a head torch.
'It's been a great day; this has been one of my favourite camps'.
'Yes, it's been a great day for reaching halfway, so sunny.'
'Let's sit here for a bit'. We sit on the rocky plateau with our backs to the tent looking up at the night sky, filled with stars. 'This is what it's all about,' I say 'This is the real world, not that of the city. This is magnificence that no man or computer can create'.

The Mountain Camp

Hopegill Head is a brilliant mountain from whichever direction you climb it. Steep and craggy with a feeling of wide-open space despite also feeling very much in the mountains. The summit is exhilarating, a sharp outcrop with steep cliff drops on one side. For a camp, the little hump south of the summit known as Sand Hill puts you right in the middle of everything and nothing at the same. We have pitched the tent on this dome and spent the evening exploring and looking down Hobcarton Crag. The 130-metre high cliff drops precipitously, and peering down from different spots makes for an exciting evening's entertainment. As the day's heat fades, we start to feel cool sitting outside the tent and make our way inside for the final night's sleep of the summer season. I'm too happy to sleep and lie inside the moonlit tent feeling wild awake.

Due for Release on 1st September 2022

Fell Asleep
Autumn – Sleeping with Wainwright

Printed in Great Britain
by Amazon